# Balut

Also Available from Bloomsbury:

*The Emergence of National Foods*, edited by Atsuko Ichijo, Venetia Johannes,
and Ronald Ranta
*Taste, Politics, and Identities in Mexican Food*, edited by
Steffan Igor Ayora Diaz
*Making Dinner*, Roblyn Rawlins and David Livert

# Balut

*Fertilized Eggs and the Making of Culinary
Capital in the Filipino Diaspora*

Margaret Magat

BLOOMSBURY ACADEMIC
LONDON • NEW YORK • OXFORD • NEW DELHI • SYDNEY

BLOOMSBURY ACADEMIC
Bloomsbury Publishing Plc
50 Bedford Square, London, WC1B 3DP, UK
1385 Broadway, New York, NY 10018, USA
29 Earlsfort Terrace, Dublin 2, Ireland

BLOOMSBURY, BLOOMSBURY ACADEMIC and the Diana logo are trademarks of
Bloomsbury Publishing Plc

First published in Great Britain 2020
This paperback edition published in 2021

Cover design by Tjaša Krivec
Cover concept: Albert Magat
Composite cover image: (Veins © Rob Jones III) & (Egg © Shongkrod Ritvichai/
EyeEm)/Getty Images

A catalogue record for this book is available from the British Library.

A catalog record for this book is available from the Library of Congress.

ISBN:  HB:    978-1-4742-8032-7
       PB:    978-1-3502-5796-2
       ePDF:  978-1-4742-8034-1
       eBook: 978-1-4742-8033-4

Typeset by Integra Software Services Pvt. Ltd.

To find out more about our authors and books visit www.bloomsbury.com
and sign up for our newsletters.

*"Probably one of the most private things in the world is an egg until it is broken"*
—M.F.K. Fisher, *How to Cook a Wolf* (1942): 53

# Contents

# List of Figures

# List of Tables

# Acknowledgments

Like many things in life, writing this book would not be possible without a community of support. To my family, especially my children Gabriel and Isabelle, who put up with my regular disappearances into the den of a library to work and my patient husband John who took care of them. For my sisters Bernadette and Kit for providing support that fueled the writing, and my niece Frannie for her technical aid. I am also indebted to Rosemary Zumwalt for her encouragement and critical feedback, and Michael Owen Jones for his advice. A special thank you to Lucy Long for her inspiring mentorship and providing a copy of her key work, *Culinary Tourism*. Nothing of course would have been possible without the steady shepherding of Miriam Cantwell and Lucy Carroll, my editors at Bloomsbury. I am most appreciative of their patience and unflagging support throughout the making of this book. Thank you also to the three anonymous reviewers, whose comments assisted in the revisions of this book. I remain grateful to all my interviewees, especially Wayne Algenio, Tita Pearl, Leo Cisneros, PJ Quesada, Arme Nicholas, and John Metzer. I wish to dedicate this work to my beloved parents, and my dearest sister Curly who passed away while I was writing this book. Thank you for the love you bestowed on me.

# Foreword: In the Light of What We Don't Know[1]

August 24, 2018
Krishnendu Ray

What could a book on *balut,* an embryonated duck egg, possibly teach us about the world we live in? Margaret Magat hopes to delineate a whisper of subversion in the face of cultural domination by taking a street food from a peripheral corner of the Philippines and tracing its circulation both nationally and globally, through various mass-mediated urban sites and diasporas, to pose sharp questions about culinary nationalism; omnivorousness, and the accumulation of cultural capital; and the role of old and new media.

Though folkloristics was one of the founding sources of food studies, it has receded from view under the glare of cultural anthropology, social history, and sociology, and thus the first compelling aspect of this book is Magat's utilization of that fecund theoretical domain.[2] Our debt to folkloristics is hidden in what is thought to be common sense. Folklore was not only one of the earliest domains of scholarly inquiry to focus on a quotidian object such as food to understand people and their relationships to each other in a spatially embedded, object-oriented way, but it also gave us a theory about why it had not been more extensively studied. Roger D. Abrahams formulated it succinctly as a "triviality barrier."[3] Out of folklore also emerges one of the earliest critiques of the fraught search for "authenticity"—that eternal question that haunts modern consumers of culture—undertaken by Regina Bendix, who links it to the discovery of the folk and their aura in nationalist historiography.[4] Yet, that search for authenticity is the very reason why documentation and analysis of everyday life emerges in the first place, allowing us to accumulate data and critique it. By pursuing the apparently trivial *balut,* Magat extends those analytical openings in the search for authentic difference, distinguishing between the *echt* and the *ersatz*—to refer back to Bendix.

In the modern Western industrial food system, life is often cellophaned away as muscle meat that cannot be put back together into the animal, while *balut* stands as a polar opposite, an unambiguous fetal life-form that we have to crunch through the beaks and proto-feathers of a baby bird to savor it. For this reason it accumulates so much baggage along the way as aphrodisiac, as delicious marker of insider Filipino palate, as disgusting food other people eat, as death on a plate, as violation of animal life, as speciesism, and so on that Magat addresses unflinchingly. Of course all organic food is death on a plate, but the nature of *balut* poses urgent questions: Where must one draw the line between sustenance and the social organization of cruelty? What can one do about extending the space between them? And should practices of minority communities be exempt from individual, moral, opprobrium? Our answers to those questions expose a vast range of cultural difference, where in spite of our apparent omnivorousness, we hesitate at the brink of both the ethical and aesthetic limits in our communities of practice. At a higher level of abstraction is another lack of consensus, and one that produces a lot of sound and fury within the social sciences: How much of what we eat is and should be collective habitual practice and how much should be the domain of individual consciousness and rationality? Whole ranges of social theoretical differences between the domains of consciousness and practice are raised by these boundary quarrels in method, theory, and belief.[5] This book on *balut* plays with both assumptions—of habituated communities of practice and of reasoned behavior toward some strategic end of domination or resistance—as productive, legitimate, and entangled alternatives.

We learn there is a gorgeous vernacularity of local taste in savoring *balut* that is unconquered by dominant scripts of cultural capital in the world. The origin of *balut*, like that of any other ordinary edible object, is unclear. It could have been a practice borrowed from the southern Chinese or from the traders of the Mekong Delta. Importantly, this is globalization prior to European hegemony that brought noodles, meat buns, and egg roll to the islands, layered over the distinctive sour palate of the pre-modern locals. Spaniards added pigs, cheeses and paella, via Mexico, reaching its apex with *adobo* that weaves together sweet, sour, spicy, and meaty into a gorgeously hybrid palate. That is spun around one more time by one of the most far-flung working-class dispersals in the modern world—the Filipino diaspora—aided by the cheapest electronic devices that reduce costs of trans-local communication and cultural exchange to almost zero. If so much is added together can we find the essence of Filipino cuisine (as a practical matter if not a theoretical one, to ask a dangerously fraught question within the anti-essentialist consensus in the humanities today)? That leads Doreen Fernandez, arguably the grand dame of Filipino cuisine in the United States, to claim that it is the condiments that make this cuisine—*calamansi* (a citrus), fish sauce (*patis*), soy sauce, vinegar, fermented shrimp paste, tart mangoes, tomatoes, etc.[6]

In any case, we find assured textual evidence of *balut,* recorded by intrepid literate outsiders, by the end of the nineteenth century among the indigenous Igorots in the Luzon highlands. By the 1950s, travelers note its ubiquity in Manila—like hotdogs in New York City. The most interesting thing I learned from this book was of *balut*'s numerous components and the ability to make distinctions among them: the "soup" of the boiled egg that you slurp through a hole relishing its intense chicken soup quality, the tough rubbery texture of the albumen you chew through, and the embryo with its beak and feathers requiring you to crunch through before finally getting to the yolk. Ideally, *balut* should be eaten about 17 days after fertilization. Then there is a range of *balut*: the *balut sa puti* with the embryo encased in the albumen; the failed *balut,* or *penoy,* with its myriad registers of good taste that may have soup or be dry, be red, yellow, or white; to the *mamatong balut* where the embryo floats on top of the yolk. What must it be to have the ability to appreciate, to have developed a palate from repeated practice, to be able to make discriminating judgments and have the linguistic capacity to comment on the qualities of a rotten, sulfuric, egg (in one variant), consumed with vinegar and garlic! This is in the adjacent domain of barbequed "adidas" (chicken feet) or grilled "helmet" (cockscomb) or smoked "IUDs" (chicken intestines) on the streets of Manila, the palate blossoming as its conjoined twin—vocabulary—proliferates. Like most premodern food, *balut* is eaten tepid not cold, seasoned with *calamansi*, vinegar, and chilies, sometimes tabasco, and downed with all forms of mind-altering substances like alcohol, hence considered transformative. This is the deep structure of local taste-making that hasn't yet been fully appropriated by great white gastronomes from the Global North, such as Andrew Zimmern or Jonathan Gold, because they lack the body-technique that includes the capacity to relish, the ability to make palatal distinctions, and the language skills of the local connoisseur, who in turn does not yet value the power of stinky cheese, the shapes of pasta, or the smelly wines of the Global North. Scholars need to follow Magat's deep dig into local vernaculars of good taste that give the global hierarchy of taste short shrift for it may teach us something new about what to eat and how to eat it with new sources of pleasure in both forms of orality, taste, and talk. That would finally take us beyond the limits of Pierre Bourdieu's analysis of cultural domination.

This little book on *balut* asks: What is it to have a cuisine spread over a 7,000-island-nation with tentacles of migrants thrown all around the world? By elaborating on a really existing nation-state with many languages and even more regions, *balut* implicitly undermines the presumption that cuisine ought to look like what came out of the courts of Byzantium or Versailles, or eighteenth-century French restaurants, or recently valorized Italian and Japanese restaurants that populate the World Top 50. In addition, it questions the even more naturalized presumption that territory is the foundation of a cuisine. In fact, the opposite may be true; water is the source of both our watersheds, which are also our foodsheds, and oceans, which may connect rather than divide, as assumed by those with abiding faith in terra firma, our ecumene. Any cuisine, including the Filipino, is a reductive palimpsest of the food of a particular class, time period, ethnicity, and location, sought to be nationalized by propaganda and profit-making moves of states and peoples. But the *balut* represents a richer repertoire of itinerant foods of peoples on the move in a world in motion and might have picked up some static as it traveled through the electronic world.

This is also a story of *aswang*: a tantalizing residue of the pre-national, pre-Western, pre-Catholic, feminized world that could not be erased in spite of all the violence of the dominant institutions of the West and the East combined. Magat reads the resonance of *balut*, seen by some as a brutal and bloodthirsty practice, as an inflection of the power of pre-colonial priestesses who posed threats to Spanish officials. They had to be demonized and thus their practice was pushed out from the domain of legitimate culture, ironically accentuating its reach as a subversive practice beyond the grasp of pedagogues and priests.

That segues nicely with the radical new work of Raj Patel and Jason Moore in *A History of the World in Seven Cheap Things* (2017). They open their chapter on Cheap Nature with the execution of an unnamed "sorceress" of Tlaxcala, New Spain on Sunday, July 18, 1599. She allegedly smashed crosses and incited Chichimec Indians to rebel, but her worst crime was dreaming of a deer riding atop a horse—the deer, symbol of Chichimec local nature, astride the colonizer's livelihood. It was judged to be seditious, challenging the cosmos of the Conquistador. Killed as a witch, the authors retell her story, a dreamer of a radically different ecology, as a balm against forgetting alternatives to capitalism's world ecology. "Our Chichimec woman," they argue, "was killed by a civilized society because her natural savagery broke its rules."[7] As recently as 1330, the authors note, savage meant valiant; that positive association faded by the end of the fifteenth century. Not coincidentally, the terms *nature* and *society* were produced as a binary, necessary to be separated, so that society's rules could be imposed on nature and anything deemed natural, such that indigenous populations, inferior races, women, and, of course, nature itself could be contained. That bad faith classification continues today, they argue, with analogous consequences. Who is the savage now, they ask pointedly? That question informs this book on *balut* too, just on a more polite register.

Magat's analysis enters the gap between the cultural commons—where things belong to everyone who has used it traditionally—and the property of a chef or a restaurant critic. She shows how a traditional object like *balut* is appropriated by outsiders (cultural orientalists, animal rights activists, big white gastronomes with good intentions in pursuit of "the great white whale of authenticity")[8] *and* insiders (Filipino chefs, cooks, and consumers at home and abroad) to make careers and arguments around culture and power. What I find particularly interesting is that she does not stop at the insider–outsider boundary but crosses it to show all kinds of conflicting behaviors by insiders and outsiders alike. Chefs Romy Dorotan and Andre Guerrero hold the *balut* at some distance so as to allow the unfamiliar customer to travel the distance from bizarre food to common difference. They eat it but they refuse to put it on their menus, refusing to sensationalize their own cuisine. The Filipino-American comedian Rex Navarrete puts it succinctly, "I want to see our cuisine on the *Food Network*, I'm tired of seeing it on *Fear Factor*" (p. 61). In contrast Chef Nicole Ponseca thrives on its notoriety and milks it for all its worth at her restaurants. I often see a long-winding line of white and not-so-white folks waiting to crack open the *balut* when I walk by one of her restaurants. That is how a $0.33 *balut* in Laguna, 56 miles south of Metro Manila, becomes a $4 *balut* at the end of its peregrinations at *Maharlika* in Manhattan.

Finally, the book is rich in object lessons about incubators with their temperatures and $CO_2$ levels, the difference between chicken and ducks—where one species needs the water physiologically while the other just plays in it—and the consequences of that in raising them profitably, the difference between mallard, Muscovy, and White Layer ducks, the sources of American *balut* south of San Francisco, how the Vietnamese like it large and hairy while the Filipinos like it petite, the source of ducks for those ubiquitous *Aflac* advertisements, etc. Along with a rich repertoire of such under-told stories and fascinating facts, I garnered about half-a-dozen important theoretical insights from this little book on *balut*. Most importantly, Magat turns the table on cultural domination by analytically cutting it open and by letting subaltern subjects speak their mind, and she does that by drawing on the theoretical literature in folkloristics, cultural sociology, and anthropology.

# Introduction

This book is an Asian American interpretation of a Western interpretation of an Asian cultural practice, specifically, the consumption of balut, or fertilized duck eggs. It was back in 2002 when I first saw balut of all places, on a top-rated American show. NBC's *Fear Factor*, Season 2, Episode 13, featured three stunts for its contestants vying to win $50,000. I couldn't believe how easy Stunt #2 was until I saw the reactions of the contestants. My elation, that a piece of Filipino culture was finally being represented on primetime television, dissolved into one of disappointment, to say the least. Seeing the revulsion and unfettered disgust from the participants on the show when confronted with the task of eating balut made me (temporarily) ashamed of being Filipino. "What was wrong with my culture?" I asked myself.

Since then, these embryonic eggs have been featured in numerous television shows, blogs, and social media. It has been labeled disgusting, weird, gross, and maligned as the number one of the most terrifying foods in the world by the website cracked.com. But balut, which is a 17- to 20-day-old duck or chicken egg eaten boiled and called *hot vit lon* by the Vietnamese, known as *pong tia koon* by Cambodians, and widely consumed throughout the rest of Southeast Asia, deserves to be understood within its proper cultural context.

A brief description of balut is necessary before further elucidation. Expanding on the above, once an egg has been fertilized, it starts to develop and can hatch into a chick after an average of 28 days. Balut refers to eggs containing partially formed embryos inside them. It is eaten boiled and not raw and is best served hot with some condiments, either salt, vinegar, or chile sauce. A typical method of eating is tapping the wide end of the egg and boring a hole in which to sip the hot liquid that tastes like concentrated chicken soup, and then peeling off the egg much like a non-fertilized hard-boiled version to eat in a few bites the yolk, embryo, and the white or the albumen, which some discard due to its rubbery texture.

The aim of this work is to set the record straight on this particular food, including its production, preparation, reception, as well as its consumption. As such it falls under the term "foodways" which folklorists such as myself use to understand "not only what people eat, but when, where, why, how and with whom" (Long 2015:13). In addition to treating this foodway using a folkloristic lens, this work investigates how the portrayal of balut with its unapologetic appearance and its consumption can illustrate identity politics and shifting cultural attitudes influenced by global migration, social media, and technology. What is it about eating balut which can garner the "intrepid" eater culinary capital? (Naccarato and LeBesco 2012). How does this translate to economic gain in the West for those with the ability to flaunt its consumption? Culinary capital refers to the prestige and social status bestowed upon individuals when they demonstrate their ability to consume or prepare food that is idealized or vilified by the surrounding culture (Naccarato and LeBesco 2012).

I am mindful of the way "identity," both the word and the concept, is much overused and comes with a heavy baggage of previous connotations and meanings from centuries past (see Abrahams 2003; Dundes [1983] 1989). "The ghosts that lie hidden in the ideological arguments of identities, nationalities, ethnicities and the other related terms need revealing" (Abrahams 2003:200), and I humbly attempt to do that in this work through the study of a particular food and its associated cultural practices. When I use the word identity, I am referring to a "persistent selfsameness" as well as a continual sharing of that selfsameness or "essential character" with others (Dundes quoting Erikson, [1983] 1989:7).

Well before balut's star turn on Western reality television in the early twenty-first century, balut or fertilized duck eggs have been enjoyed in the Philippines since at least the nineteenth century (M. Duval 1885; Roberts 1837), if not earlier. Declared as "the national street food of the Philippines" (Fernandez 1994), and eaten as a humble street food or portable snack, balut is widely consumed by children, adults, and elders throughout Southeast Asia. This traditional delicacy is similar in taste to a hard-boiled egg except that in addition to the yolk and the albumen, there is a partially developed chick inside, with a beak and a few feathers. In the Philippines as well as many Filipino American homes, these snacks are usually consumed with family and friends, in a social gathering such as parties or drinking sessions. It is also eaten as an energy booster for those who are fatigued and hungry, recommended as a high-protein food for students, and touted as a calcium-rich superfood for pregnant women and invalids. In the United States. and in the Philippines, balut is particularly known as the "Filipino Viagra" by men of Filipino heritage and increasingly by other men of different ancestries who consume the fertilized eggs as a rumored aphrodisiac.

But balut as portrayed in the West is a hair-raising attraction to be "conquered" in various news and travel segments featuring celebrity chefs like Andrew Zimmern, Gordon Ramsay, and Anthony Bourdain. Since its debut in traditional media, balut has emerged to be a bonafide internet star featured in many videos, blogs, and selfies in the last two decades. Indeed, the challenge of eating this delicacy with what is essentially a young chick inside has created an online cottage industry where money is to be made depending on the number of clicks. Online videos range from 30,000 to over 10 million views of first-time consumers trying this food. Although traditionally enjoyed in intimacy with family and friends, amateur shows featuring balut and its torn-apart components are now watched by a worldwide audience. What has taken it from relative obscurity to be a viral attraction?

This book focuses on the consumption of balut in the contexts where the eater is consciously eating it in her/his search for "self-realization." It provides the traditional context of this foodway before delving into an examination of how it is being contemporarily used as a cultural practice which gives consumers from a Filipino ancestry the agency to be a "real Filipino" no matter where one is located in the Philippine diaspora. It also explores how others from various backgrounds use balut to boost their claim to be entitled foodies (Naccarato and LeBesco 2012; Warde et al. 1999).

Balut's ability to garner culinary capital may have played a major role in its transformation into a reality television favorite and lead character in many a YouTube video. From the cultural practice of daring newcomers or returning Filipinos to eat balut in the Philippines (see Matejowsky 2013), to the new tradition in "balut challenge" videos where individuals from all backgrounds are urged to consume it or gleefully film themselves eating balut, balut become a food with the power to delineate eaters to become instant ' "citizens" and savvy cosmopolitan foodies (Warde et al. 1999).

Balut, like other globalized Asian foods such as kimchi and sushi, helps illustrate the artificial binary evident in the discussion of culinary authenticity (see Ji-Song Ku 2013). But in contrast to other foods that are deemed "authentic" in the method of preparation or produced in a place of undeniable origin, balut is as close to an "authentic" food as one can get (although authenticity itself is a constructed illusion) (Bendix 1997; Ku 2013). One cannot mask the fact that to eat a balut is to eat an embryonic duck or chicken complete with feathers and a beak.

Unlike other foods, balut's main attraction is its original, unvarnished appearance which instantly "authenticates" its consumers. Therein lies a main component of its appeal, whether one is manipulating the food as a symbol of national identity as a Filipino or forcing it down one's throat in a bid to demonstrate bravado in conquering what many consider as a "bizarre" food, to say the least. Ways of consuming the fertilized egg may vary, but once harvested, the balut chick is forever in the state of halted formation. As such, it is the reason why eaters will use it to separate the "authentic" eater from others.

I suggest that balut's unapologetic, no-holds barred appearance, deemed by many as "genuine" Filipino cuisine, may be used and manipulated for cultural and culinary capital in today's experience economy. For others of non-Filipino heritage, eating balut becomes a way to conquer the Other in an attempt to prove that one is a cosmopolitan omnivore (Warde et al. 1999). It is a feat that can garner one culinary capital that can easily be turned into economic profit (Naccarato and LeBesco 2012). This is done by aspiring foodies and reality television producers who feed the audience need for reality-based gore, obliging their viewers with a bit-by-bit description and depiction of the eating of the egg, including the common sight of sudden regurgitation to boot.

Defining identity through the use of a cultural practice or folklore (Dundes [1983] 1989) is a key topic of this work, which is influenced by my background in the field of folklore, known as folkloristics, and Asian American studies. The folk in question are those of Filipino ancestry as well as others drawn to the cultural practice of eating balut, or the "lore" of the folk. The folk can be "any group whatsoever who share at least one common factor" (Dundes 1965:2).

This idea of the folk moves away from the trap of relying simply on an "ethnic identity" because there are many group and personal identities and it is more useful to think of a group sharing "a common core of traditions"

(Dundes [1983] 1989:11). The expressive practice of eating balut, now affiliated to American popular culture as well as to traditional Filipino culture, can be analyzed using the term "folkloric identity" (Zhang 2015) which extends Dundes's seminal definition.

Although long ignored by other fields, the field of food studies is now increasingly seen as critical in the understanding of a culture, including its history, sociopolitical and historical contexts. Food studies demand an interdisciplinary focus and folkloristics is particularly well suited to the examination of food, both its symbolic and material aspects. Born out of the marriage of anthropology and literature since its inception as a field over a hundred years ago (Bendix 1997; Zumwalt 1988), folkloristics with its interdisciplinary status offers an advantage in the study of food. Folklorists have long examined food's role in culture, ethnicity, performance, and gender (see, e.g., Anderson 1971; Camp 1980, 1989; Georges 1984; Goode et al. 1984; Jones 1981; Kalcik 1984; Kirshenblatt-Gimblett 1991; Magliocco 1993; Staub 1989; Theophano 1982, 1991; Yoder 1972). The use of food to construct and negotiate identity has also been covered in various folklore studies (see, e.g., Gutierrez 1984; Humphrey and Humphrey 1988; Jones 2005; Lockwood and Lockwood 2000; Long 2009; Yoder 1972) with entire journals dedicated to food studies like *Digest: A Journal of Foodways & Culture* which began in 1977 and still remains an active publication. There are special editions devoted to the topic, such as the *Journal of American Folklore*'s winter 2009 issue dedicated to the topic of "Food and Identity in Americas" and whole anthologies containing analyses from folklorists including Brown and Mussell 1984 and Jones and Long 2017. Because folklorists study culture—from the material to the intangible practices that are meaningful for communities all over the world—they are particularly suited as food scholars to shed insight on why people eat what they do.

Not surprisingly, the nascent field of food studies draws a majority of its inspiration from folklore studies (Long 2015:1). Some key works from folklorists that continue to be relevant to food studies research include a 1981 article by Simon Bronner which noted the often-conflicting food behaviors of individuals and how researchers need to analyze food attitudes as variable and not static (Bronner 1981:121). Contradictory food-related behaviors need not be reconciled by the researcher but examined fully to illustrate the complexities and multiple reasons why individuals eat the foods they do "even if or when they eat these things with mixed feelings of pride and loathing" (Bronner 1981:124). This is the case for balut which incites paradoxical feelings of ethnic identification as well as revulsion. Writing about the Italian American preference and consumption of such "exotic" dishes as goats' heads in Mormon Utah, Richard Raspa theorizes that such consumption may enable "the communicant to partake of the power of the ingested creature" (1984:193). This is directly related to balut, where an eater is basically ingesting the life force of a chick which represents rebirth. Yvonne and William Lockwood examine the history and tradition of "pasties" in Michigan's Upper Peninsula, illustrating the importance of this meat-filled pastry to this region and also how it reveals that the cultural practices of an ethnic group is influenced by other factors besides the culture of the mother country (1998:21). Other critical works by folklorists include Roger Abrahams's work where he argues as "equal opportunity eaters," we can eat anything once which can lead to the exploitation of others via cultural appropriation of their foods (Abrahams 1984:23), and Michael Owen Jones's edited volume of food habits which directed research (1981). Lucy Long's concept of culinary tourism (2004) remains especially useful in contemporary food studies that deal with the intersection of food adventurism along with issues of cultural food colonialism and appropriation.

With the rising popularity of balut contests, whether online or in festivals, I explore how the concept of folkloric identity is suited to describe such events. In doing so, it is my intention to move away from racial/ethnic-based studies of lore toward analysis of expressive practices occurring in diasporic, transnational contexts by people who may or may not be affiliated with a specific population. Balut, although traditionally eaten in the company of friends and family, has now moved to a more visible stage as a symbolic marker of identity (as well as Other-ness), performed in part by mirroring portrayals in social media and reality television.

This work's focus is to understand the performances of culinary capital by those who are Filipino Americans as well as those outside of that population. How do these differ, and what drives and motivates such cultural practices? Whether in online videos, traditional use, or in festivals, the common factor seems to be the use of the fertilized duck eggs and the mining of reactions to the eating of this fare. By examining the phenomena related to this Southeast

Asian delicacy, it is my intention to illustrate how the forces of postcolonialism, migration, technology, and nationalism have all converged and contributed to the meteoric rise and popularity of this oft-misunderstood delicacy.

Imagination and the role it plays in the everyday life are also covered in this work. Electronic media and mass migration have compelled the work of the imagination (Appadurai 1996) and the practice of eating balut whether online or in festivals is a practice of the modern. In examining balut's presence in "diasporic public spheres" and mediascapes (Appadurai 1996:10), one can see how all sorts of subjectivities are formed, whether it results in a type of culinary citizenship or a kind that interweaves reality television, the Travel Channel and images of culinary celebrities all in one. Through the focus on balut consumption, this work provides one glimpse of how the imagination is exerted in the twenty-first century as it is influenced by globalization, migration, and the electronic media (Appadurai 1996).

The book also takes up the issues confronted by scholars of Asian American culture. In studies about Asian American foodways, it has been pointed out that "social, political, economic, and historical forces, as well as power inequalities, including discriminatory immigration and land laws, have circumscribed Asians materially and symbolically in the alimentary realm" (Ku et al. 2013:1). Through the focus on one specific foodway, this work traces how the trajectory of the consumption as well as reception of this one particular food can display the interplay of sociopolitical and economic experience of Filipino migrants and shed light on the historical experience many have had in the United States and the growing interest in Filipino cuisine as "the next big thing" (as uttered by Andrew Zimmern in 2012).

I also look at how the taste for such so-called exotic fare can illustrate what Edward Said noted in *Orientalism* (1978). Said identifies the colonial oppression of the Other, where the East is compared and contrasted in favor of the West in academic discourse, literature, and the arts. However, rather than subscribe to a simple binary distinction, I aim to depict the complexities of how the Western reception of foods like balut is manipulated and utilized by those from the Filipino population as well as from other backgrounds. The image of the passive "ethnic" being taken advantage of by the white colonizer is contested/challenged/overturned by the ways that the Other is talking back and provided agency by using traditional food as bait to entice non-

Filipinos to eat Filipino cuisine. The lure of the culinary capital promised by the "conquest" of such food is too much for many an omnivorous eater, who then succumbs to devouring balut as an attempt to differentiate themselves and obtain bragging rights as an intrepid foodie. This attraction to exotic foods is being used by savvy Filipino American entrepreneurs who capitalize on the thirst for unfamiliar fare.

In addition to folkloristic and anthropological studies, as well as Asian American perspectives, my approach to this work is informed by my background as a Filipino American from a family of foodies. Born and raised in the Philippines before immigrating in my early teens to Los Angeles, California, I grew accustomed to a landscape full of diverse cultures and cuisines. However, Filipino food did not strike a nerve in mainstream media until only lately. I had been aware of the cultural practice of eating balut from my childhood and fieldwork in the 1990s which produced an article, but my interest in delving into it was sparked by the increasingly outrageous portrayals of balut-eating in both traditional and social media.

For this book, I conducted semi-structured interviews with individuals familiar with the making and selling of balut as well as those who promote the food and eat it (see Appendix for interview questions). Among those I interviewed included a duck farmer, balut distributors, a balut vendor as well as balut-eaters. I also conducted an online survey. In addition, I observed two balut-eating contests and interviewed several participants and organizers. Using participant observation, I did fieldwork in two California farmers' markets and one flea market in San Jose, California. My fieldwork is supplemented with observations of popular culture, from television reality shows to YouTube channels and social media blogs to articles in the news media.

To understand the power of how a simple street food in Southeast Asia is manipulated by many in the West on their quest to remake the Self requires an explanation of the background of this foodway. Chapter 1 delves into the historical and traditional contexts of balut production and consumption. It introduces the reader to the history of balut and its use in Filipino culture and society and provides details of fieldwork with a duck farmer and those involved in its distribution. Chapter 2 looks at the notion of balut as representing the Other, from being used as a "tool of oppression" to now being embraced as an identity marker. I examine balut's role in the culinary nationalism that has swept the Filipino food movement to the forefront to become the latest *menu du jour*. Culinary nationalism refers to when "food and cuisine are tied to place" (Ferguson 2010:105). In Chapter 3, I discuss its connection to supernatural lore and the legends of the *aswang*, who may be seen as similar to the Western notion of a vampire. I also examine the psychological factors of eating balut, including the symbolism of the egg and the cultural belief that balut is an aphrodisiac and a natural "Viagra." In Chapter 4, I examine balut-eating contests through the lens of performance theory from the folklore discipline, drawing from fieldwork conducted in San Francisco's Annual Balut Eating Contest each August. This section asks questions such as what lures people to watch balut eating? What motivates the contest sponsors and what makes the contestants participate? How is Filipino identity being performed? Chapter 5 illustrates the popular depiction of balut in reality television, travel shows, and food blogs, supplemented by data from recent study participants. It highlights the ways that balut has been manipulated as an identity marker for those who want to be Filipino or be seen as "Filipino," and how it is also used as a test for "courage" or eating bravura. The concluding chapter poses the question of what the reception of this food can reveal about the current status of Filipino Americans in the United States and how it can serve as an indicator of what lies ahead for them, as well as for others who are drawn into the debate of culinary authenticity and nationalism.

1

# Why Eat Balut? Consumption and Tradition

While balut entered the popular imaginary of the West only fairly recently, it has long been a part of the Philippines' culture. In *The History of Mankind* (1896–1898), geographer Friedrich Ratzel describes that "the Tagals are said to have learnt from the Chinese to eat eggs that have been sat upon, with the chick in them, as tit-bits" (1896–1898:432; as cited in Magat 2002). The indigenous Igorots, who live in the highlands of Luzon, Philippines, were noted as eating eggs that have been developed, or "until there is something in the egg to eat" (Jenks 1905:143).

By the 1950s, balut was as ubiquitous in Manila much like "hotdogs" in the United States (Maness 1950:10), and it was hailed as the "national passion" (Mydans 1997). It is now found widely beyond the Luzon region and sold throughout the Philippines such as the Visayas and in the southern region of Mindanao (Reyes-Estrope 2017).

What has taken balut from its relative obscurity as an ordinary street food to be a famous attraction in the West? What are the factors that have influenced its popularity? This chapter situates the cultural practice of eating balut within its traditional and historical contexts. Fieldwork conducted in a duck farm and farmers' markets as well as interviews with balut producers and distributors provide a picture of balut production and distribution in the United States. In examining the cultural factors involved in eating balut, this chapter sets up the subsequent chapters that investigate why balut consumption has become such a visible, often-contested act in the United States.

## The egg and its contents

Most everyone is familiar with the unfertilized egg, that when boiled, results in a solid yolk and a soft white albumen. A balut egg, in contrast, is a fertilized egg that has a growing embryo inside it. When boiled for about 20 minutes, a 17-day-old balut egg, as it is preferred by Filipinos, has four noticeable components: the soup or broth, the yolk, the embryo, and the white or hard albumen. To consume it properly, one first taps the wide part of the egg to crack a hole in the shell. After peeling off the shell and membrane, the soup is sipped before the egg is further peeled and the entire egg is eaten in two or three bites. Sometimes, the albumen or white part of the egg (called *bato* or rock for its tough and rubbery texture) is discarded but it is edible. Depending on the age of the balut egg, the embryo may already have discernible feathers, bones, and a beak. One can tell a balut egg is fresh if the liquid broth is still present. If not, that egg is most likely old or dried up. The majority of my online respondents describe balut as delicious, with the broth tasting like "intense chicken soup."

The embryo or chick is relatively a tiny one at 17 days, the preferred stage for Filipinos. There is hardly a feather or any hard bones that are felt at this stage. The older the balut, the more the embryo is developed with a more defined beak, head, and feathers. The perfect balut is *balut sa puti* (egg in white) where the embryo is wrapped in the albumen and unseen when one first cracks open the balut. The other kind of balut is *mamatong balut* where the embryo "floats" on top of the yolk and the hard albumen. In *mamatong balut*, one is confronted with the bird from the beginning, which may explain why traditionally, Filipinos eat the balut quickly and not linger over looking at it. It is said that one way to tell if a balut is *mamatong balut* would be to drop it in a bowl of water to see if it floats. If it rests on the surface of the water, then it is believed to be a *mamatong balut*, and if it sinks, then it is thought to be *balut sa puti*.

Balut is best eaten warm and not cold, with a twist of salt or splash of vinegar, chile, or with herbs the way it is enjoyed in Vietnam and Cambodia. It is meant to be eaten with friends and family or in a social setting where drinks such as beer and other alcoholic beverages are available. These drinking sessions are called "*inuman*" in the Philippines and one normally serves balut as a *pulutan* (appetizer) in these kinds of events. This social aspect of eating balut is confirmed by the majority of my online respondents who ate balut with others.

Influenced by Chinese medicine, balut is considered by Filipinos to be a "hot" food that will increase the *yang* and raise the *qi*. Therefore, it is not prescribed for individuals suffering from fever. Some of my interviewees also noted its high cholesterol amount. But others like balut distributor Butch Coyoca believe that balut is a "powerbar, a superfood" that compensates with vitamins for those who are not sleeping enough (Magat 2002).

Although balut is usually consumed as a snack or *pulutan*, it can also be served as a dish with rice. It can be put inside dough and baked in a ramekin as it was prepared in the Philippines, or fried in garlic with lots of butter as it is done in Matthew's Grill, a popular restaurant in Gaithersburg, Maryland. The presence of balut has been documented in Greenland and in places as diverse as Sydney, Rome, and Prague; in short, wherever Southeast Asians, especially Filipinos, work and congregate as one of the largest diasporic populations.

In 2019, the Philippines's population was estimated to be about 109 million, and its capital is Manila (Figure 1). Described as the world's most densely populated city with about 46,000 people per square mile (Weller 2016), more than 12 million live in the greater Metro Manila area. Imposing skyscrapers and air-conditioned megamalls packed with luxury goods command attention and invite consumption while numerous shanties and poverty-stricken communities are evidence of the uneven economic development in this predominantly Christian country.

About 11 percent of Filipinos work as Overseas Filipino Workers (OFWs) in over 100 countries. The top 10 countries are the United States, Saudi Arabia, United Arab Emirates, Malaysia, Canada, Australia, Italy, United Kingdom, Qatar, and Singapore, and Figure 2 provides estimates of the number of OFWs in those respective countries. Overall, the diaspora population of OFWs is estimated to be twice the population of New Zealand (Gonzalez 2012:16). In 2017, OFWs sent back an estimated $28.1 billion in remittances (Cuaresma 2018). A visible product of those remittances can be seen, for example, in new subdivisions in Batangas where mansions with Roman columns and gleaming marble were built with the funds from those OFWs working and living in Italy (Magat 2003).

As testament to the cosmopolitan experiences and tastes of its citizens, food of all kinds can be found in Manila. From the best Spanish tapas restaurants to Mediterranean eateries, hamburger chains to shawarmas on the go, Filipinos are familiar with foods from around the world. "The country's food taste are now shaped by a transnational population proud of its regional culinary

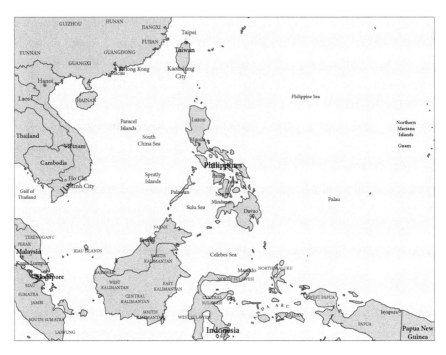

**Figure 1** Map of the Philippines.

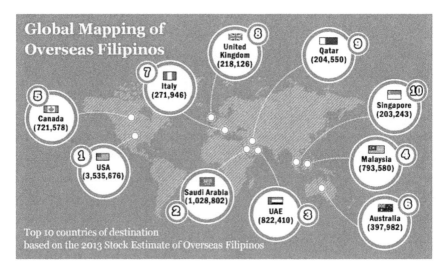

**Figure 2** Map showing Filipino diasporic population in top 10 countries—Courtesy of Commission on Filipinos Overseas.

traditions and open to new ideas brought to the country by overseas foreign workers" (Orquiza 2013:184).

In addition to the variety in cuisines, regional variation is evident within the archipelago. Three main regions of Luzon, Visayas, and Mindanao are known for particular dishes. In Ilocos Norte, in Luzon, *pinakbet* makes use of bitter melon and fermented shrimp paste, while spicy chilies and coconut milk are enjoyed in Bicol in the Visayas region (Magat 2015). In Mindanao, both Indian and Arab influences are evident with the heavy use of spices (Fernandez 2003:65). But some dishes such as *adobo, sinigang,* and *kinilaw* are found throughout, albeit with variations in preparation and ingredients. A favorite snack, balut is one of those foods that can also be found all over the Philippines, despite its past history when it was eaten more in Luzon (Lopez 1986:363).

Balut is a food of the everyday and has now arguably become a dish identified with the Philippines, despite its consumption throughout Southeast Asia. This is because balut is found "all the time and everywhere—on streets, at stalls, outside movie houses, outside nightclubs and discos, in markets; by vendors walking, sitting, or squatting; at midnight and early dawn, at breakfast, lunch, merienda, and dinner time" (Fernandez 1994:10).

No matter if the setting is urban or rural, balut can be easily be procured in the Philippines. In transport centers in the city, where a high rate of customers is vying to catch a crowded bus or jeepney, balut vendors hawk their wares in the spaces where people jostle on their way to catch rides. In the rural areas, balut vendors wander the streets and call out in a sing-song voice that they have balut. The urban areas also now have balut in expensive malls (Figure 3), whereas in the rural provinces, it can easily be found in a sari-sari (mixed-mixed or variety store) that caters to locals. As one heads out of Manila city into the countryside, balut can be found in the commercial plazas that have sprouted along the highways, where one can fuel up on gas and food.

As of May 2018, during a trip to the Philippines, I noted the average price of 17 pesos to 20 pesos per balut egg, or 33–38 cents at the current exchange rate. This makes the $4.00 price tag per balut egg in New York restaurants particularly eyebrow-raising. Balut is sold by itself or with salted eggs, which have traditionally been eaten with tomatoes and onions as a type of salad or used as a topping for *bibingka* (a type of rice cake). Salted duck eggs have

**Figure 3** Organic balut by Green Babes in the Philippines.

made its way into flavoring potato chips and being featured on "*putopao,*" a hybrid combining *puto* (another type of rice cake) with *siopao* (*char sui bao,* or meat bun).

Despite the decline of the balut industry in Pateros, a municipality in the Metro Manila area, balut is still tied to its reputation. Pateros is now mostly a residential area, however, and there are plans by the municipal government to buy incubators for its residents as an attempt to reinvigorate the balut-making tradition (De Guzman 2017). The fact remains that access to clean water is what ducks need and Pateros no longer has that. Balut vendors can still be found in Pateros but they obtain their eggs elsewhere (De Guzman 2017).

Balut remains a part of the cultural landscape as well as the soundscape of the Philippines. At night, in local neighborhoods or around nightclubs, bars, or transportation centers, one hears the howling call from vendors advertising its availability. Each vendor would often have his/her own style of calling "bal-uuuut!" which can vary from person to person. The balut eggs are carried in baskets covered with materials to keep the eggs warm. They are served with a twist of salt, along with other condiments such as vinegar and chile. In short, balut can be readily obtained whenever a speedy, protein-filled snack is needed.

The hawking cadence of the "balut" call has been parodied in songs and YouTube videos, but it is a part of Filipino culture that has not translated to the United States where balut is sold in farmers' markets, Asian grocery stores, and duck farms like Metzer Farms in Gonzales, California. The one exception I know about is of a New York restaurant that provides balut accompanied by the servers calling out "ba-luut!" whenever a patron orders the dish.

A brief foray into the geography and history of the Philippines is essential to understand the influences of what is now called Filipino cuisine. More than anything, it is a record of the historical trading, 300-plus years of colonization, as well as the contemporary influences that have left marks on the dishes that have become "Filipinized" through the process of indigenization via modes of preparation, condiments, and local ingredients (Fernandez 2003).

## Philippines: geography and history

The Philippine archipelago is made up of over 7,000 islands with terrain composed of mountains, streams, valleys, and bays that influence regional varieties in cuisine. Only about a thousand islands are inhabited and its coastline is measured at 36,289 kilometers long. From the northern tip of the Ilocos region to about a thousand miles to the south to Mindanao, the archipelago contains an astonishing variety of endemic species, animals as well as plants. For example, more than 100 endemic mammal species live in the Philippines, including the Philippine tarsier. In some areas of Luzon and Mindanao, the topography is 25 million years old while other parts of the country are estimated to be 100,000 to 10 million years old (Francia 2010:25).

Little is known about the natives who occupied pre-colonial Philippines as they relied on oral tradition and documents which were written were destroyed by the Spanish. The oldest written document that has been found in the Philippines is the Laguna Copper-Plate Inscription, dated 900 CE. Discovered in 1989 by a worker near the mouth of the Lumbang River in Laguna, the copper plate writing, a debt acquittal, included Sanskrit and old Malay languages. It proved that the country or at least a part of it had an organized customary law system in place some 600 years before Spanish colonization, and that there was a thriving relationship with Java and other nearby kingdoms (Postma 1992). By the tenth century, China had become a trading partner as well (Scott 1989).

The first time Westerners set eyes on the archipelago was on March 16, 1521, when the Portuguese explorer named Ferdinand Magellan under the employ of the Spanish caught sight of the island of Leyte, in the Visayas region (Karnow 1989:34; Rafael 2000). Magellan had been in search of spices, and he also intended to convert natives to Christianity. Magellan was able to erect a cross and baptize some 2,000 residents of the island of Cebu before losing his life to Lapulapu, a chief on the island of Mactan. Magellan was followed by other *conquistadors*, and in 1543, the Spanish explorer Ruy López de Villalobos christened the archipelago *Filipinas*, after the Spanish crown prince who later became King Felipe II (Philip II) (Francia 2010:10; Rafael 2000:5). By 1565, Miguel Lopez de Legazpi set up the settlement of Cebu (Rafael 2000:5), which to this day, continues to carry visible remnants of its Spanish legacy through its buildings and people more than any other city in the Philippines.

By the time the Spanish arrived in sixteenth-century Manila, Chinese merchants were already conducting business in the area (Karnow 39). But the Spanish could have lost to other colonial powers. In 1646, only two aging Spanish galleons mostly manned by Filipinos were available to fend off the Dutch and their 19 warships. This event is celebrated in the Philippines in the Feast of Our Lady of La Naval, as many credit her divine intercession for the victory over the Dutch. Besides the Dutch, the British briefly owned the archipelago in 1762–1764, if not for the Spanish winning back control (Rafael 2000).

From 1570 when Legazpi made Manila the capital of the Philippines until around 1898 when Spain lost to the United States in the Spanish-American War, the general population of Filipinos served as menials under a small minority of the Spanish colonial officials, friars, and native-born nobles (Ileto 1979; Karnow 1989). As the Philippines was opened up to foreign trade in 1834, other foreigners succeeded in owning tracts of land. Descendants of these landowners intermarried with Chinese mestizos and other mixed-blood settlers and their descendants remain rich property owners even today (see Karnow 1989).

During the three centuries of Spanish rule, Filipinos were conscripted or forced into labor by the Spanish. With the exception of chiefs and their oldest sons, every single Filipino male was ordered to serve for at least 40 days each year in construction of roads and transportation systems, as well as to labor in the procurement of raw materials such as wood and transporting these as well as other materials from the mountains to the coasts (Alegado 1992:154). In addition, *indios* or Manilamen (as Filipinos were also called) served in the Spanish naval and army forces, and they traveled throughout the world onboard the Spanish galleons (Alegado 1992). This type of forced migration could be seen as the first of four types of Philippine migration.

The other three kinds of migration include Filipinos who were recruited to work in California and Hawai'i, voluntary migration by intellectual Filipinos who left for Spain, and refugee migration (Alegado 1992:154). Of particular relevance to this work is the early-twentieth-century migration of Filipinos who were recruited to work in American farms and canneries, as this group helped build the foundation of Filipino American foodways in the United States, as it will be explained later in Chapter 2.

The first written record of Filipinos stepping foot on what is now known as American soil occurred in 1587, when a Spanish galleon docked in Morro Bay, California. The four *Luzones* (Filipinos from the Luzon region) disembarked to stake land in the name of Spain. Two of the men were reported to have been killed and the remaining two escaped (Pido 1997:21).

In 1763, a group of "Manilamen" fled from Spanish galleons and settled in Louisiana (Takaki 1989:315), intermarrying with Cajuns and influencing the shrimp drying technology which was adapted in the region. In Alaska, a Filipino seaman was recorded to have arrived in 1788 on a merchant ship trading for fur (Buchholdt 1996) and in Acapulco, Mexico, many more Filipino males deserted galleons, married Mexican women, and settled into Mexican society or made their way to California (Espina 1988).

For the majority of those who remained in the Philippines, however, life was made difficult by the fact that vast amounts of land were claimed by the Catholic Church and the rich landowners were a few Castilian-Filipino families, Chinese businessmen, and Spanish officials (Eviota 1992; Karnow 1989). By the late eighteenth century, when Spain competed with England's

Industrial Revolution by increasing Philippine production of hemp, sugar, and tobacco, landless Filipinos became a familiar sight.

Noted historian Vicente Rafael charges that the Philippines was in effect "doubly colonized, belonging to Spain (and until 1821, administered as a Mexican province through the trade connection between Manila and Acapulco) but also to the expansive geography of a world capitalist system that stretched across the Pacific and Atlantic Oceans" (Rafael 2000:5). Rafael argues that the Philippine colony was connected to overseas markets run by British, North American, and German merchants who owned stakes in railroads and sugar plantations. From this "agricultural revolution," a middle class of "mestizo" (mixed race) arose, which included those *ilustrados* like national hero Jose Rizal who helped foment nationalist fever (Rafael 2000:5).

The living situation of many Filipinos continued to worsen in the nineteenth century, with families forced to seek for food from village to village and whatever land to cultivate. By the 1880s, anger against the Spanish cultivated a growing patriotism (Ileto 1979; Jose 1992; Rafael 2000). The Philippine society was divided into few classes, with the Spanish officials and landowners at the top along with their local Filipino allies, while situated at the lowest class were the rest of Filipinos who were removed from their land and means to sustain themselves. In effect, a whole class of dispossessed Filipinos had developed who were now compelled to sell their labor (Eviota 1992:60).

From the 1840s to 1910, small mutinies would take place, fueled by the folk revolting first against the Spanish clergy (Ileto 1979), then later followed by protests against the American officials who had come to enforce the policy of "benevolent assimilation" as proclaimed by US President McKinley in 1898. During the end of the nineteenth century and the beginning of the twentieth, the Philippines was gripped with an economic depression and stifling bureaucracy along with the widespread abuses of Spanish clergy and officials against Filipinos (Karnow 1989). These factors drove national hero Jose Rizal's patriotic writings and folklorist Isabelo de los Reyes's efforts to propagate indigenous folklore and history, helping create "an imagined nation" (Anderson [1983] 1991).

But the Spanish control did not extend to all of the archipelago, as areas of the archipelago including the northern part of the Cordillera, parts of the Visayas, and the southern region of Mindanao and Sulu "clearly stood on the periphery of colonial control," where one could dodge the colonial hold (Rafael 2000:6). These places remained the least-influenced areas of the Spanish colonialization.

Spain, and then the United States paved the way for the Philippines to take part in the global export market. But it was a lopsided development which resulted in enormous disparities between class and gender and led to women being marginalized from economic life (Eviota 1992: vi). The emphasis on crops for export such as tobacco and sugar ruined the local economy of the regions and caused the demise of most subsistence farming (Eviota 1992:47; Karnow 1989). Analyzing books, poems, testimonies, and stories, feminist scholar Nadia Tadiar agrees with Eviota that skills and labor was "gendered" but expands to further note that the feminization of labor is "the realization of a historical tendency" (Tadiar 2009:33). This is reflected in more Filipina women working as OFWs than Filipino men, according to the Philippine Statistics Authority in 2017.

With the defeat of Spain in the Spanish-American War in 1898, the United States took over as the dominant force, and the events of "invasion, torture, reconcentration, deportation and murder" which marked the beginning of American colonization were omitted in favor of a narrative that situated the Americans "as the true heirs of the revolution which faltered in the hands of elite Filipinos" (Rafael 2002:368). Two years earlier, the Philippine Revolution movement against Spain had begun in 1896 with several events: the formation of the Katipunan, a secret society headed by revolutionary hero Andres Bonifacio, the takeover of Cavite by rebel leader and later first president Emilio Aguinaldo, and the execution of Jose Rizal at the hands of Spanish authorities. But Spain did not capitulate or recognize the Filipino independence, and it only surrendered to the Americans under the Treaty of Paris which gave Cuba its independence, while ceding Puerto Rico and Guam to the United States and stipulating that $20 million be given for the Philippines (see Shaw and Francia 2002).

The nationalist writings of Jose Rizal and the "father" of Philippine folklore Isabelo de Los Reyes were borrowed by American colonial officials and scholars, along with the native folklore so that American imperialism was legitimized (Rafael 2003). Paternalism justified American presence and helped spread the image of the inept Filipino. All of these factors combined to "repress" the illegitimacy of the American presence in the Philippines (Rafael

2003:36). What began as the Philippine Revolution in 1896 continued as the Philippine-American War between Filipino nationalists and American troops sent on their mission of imperialism. The Philippine-American War is officially recorded as beginning on 1898 and lasting until 1902, but some scholars have contended that it lingered, to 1912 if not longer (Ileto 1979; Rafael 2003).

What does this history have to do with balut? As will be shown, this complicated relationship with the United States continues to color the treatment of Filipino Americans and their experiences as immigrants to America. Whether American officials were depicting Filipinos as "little brown brothers" in need of guidance from the United States or as "savages" who needed to be civilized as they were portrayed in the St. Louis Expo of 1904 (Grindstaff 1999), the American colonial period in the Philippines was marked with sweeping reform geared toward United States' interests. During the first 50 years of the twentieth century, for example, American reformers manipulated public education and geared food advertisements and cookbooks toward cultivating consumerist desires for Western goods, resulting in the devaluation of Filipino food (Orquiza 2013:177).

American foods were seen as sophisticated and Filipino dishes were described as "primitive" and the people who ate them as "vindictive and treacherous" (Orquiza 178; quoting Jose de Olivares in 1899). This degradation of Filipino people and their food may well be the origin of the inferiority complex stemming from colonialism which resulted in the shame or *hiya* many Filipinos in America feel when it comes to the foods they eat, such as balut (Shah 2014). Along with this "hiya," the appearance and texture of balut are factors that make its public consumption even more meaningful for Filipino Americans, as will be argued in later chapters.

## The history of balut production and its role in Filipino foodways

For centuries, the production of balut in the Philippines was associated with a village called Pateros, located in the shores of Laguna de Bay, a freshwater lake about 40 kilometers from Manila (Magat 2002; Maness 1950:10–13). In 1834, Edmund Roberts, named as a "special agent" for the United States who was dispatched to Asia to negotiate trade, visited Pateros and referred to it as "Duck-Town" due to the many ducks that were being raised by the villagers (Roberts 1837:60–61).

It is likely that the name is derived from Spanish, as it means "duck-raisers" (Maness 1950). The ducks fed on snails from the lake, producing balut that had a clean taste, perhaps enhanced by the traditional incubation of the eggs using heated rice husks that gave the egg a sweet taste, according to the narratives related by my interviewees.

By 1950, Pateros's balut industry had 400,000 ducks producing eggs (Maness 1950) out of an estimated 700,000 plus ducks that existed in the Philippines at that time (Chang and Dagaas 2004). Twenty years later, however, production had diminished due to pollution in the Laguna de Bay and balut producers moved elsewhere (Magat 2002). Places like Zamboanga and Bulacan outside Manila now manufacture balut. The municipality of Victoria, Laguna located 56 miles south of Metro Manila is now known as the "Duck Raising Center of the Philippines" (De Guzman 2017). At the end of April each year, the town holds an "Itik Festival" complete with parades and other festivities. The word "itik" is Tagalog for "duck" and it also refers to the type of duck that originated in Pateros, according to the website of the Cadiz Duck Farm which is located in Victoria, Laguna. Farms like Cadiz Duck Farm are the ones who are now supplying duck eggs to Pateros to be sold in greater Manila. Business is booming outside of Pateros for the rest of those in the duck industry, with demand for salted and balut eggs remaining high (De Guzman 2017). In 2017, however, a ban on balut production due to the bird flu resulted in a price increase for sellers in Mindanao and the Visayas (Reyes-Estrope 2017). This ban was only a temporary one.

There are very few scholarly works that exist regarding embryonic eggs, with most comprised of short mentions that tend to be descriptive (see, e.g., Simoons 1961). Filipino food scholar Doreen Fernandez provided an invaluable interpretation of balut in its cultural contexts and noted a range of preparation and possibilities between the unhatched duckling and the fully formed chick (1994, 1996a, b). I wrote an expanded treatment of balut and the sociocultural factors that influence its consumption (Magat 2002), while anthropologist Ty Matejowsky discussed balut's liminality and how it can constitute a rite-of-passage for outsiders (2013).

My research into the history of balut and its origins revealed that China may have been the place where balut originated. The partially developed eggs were once reserved for people from the upper classes (Crawfurd 1830:408). These are still eaten and called *máo jī dàn* according to my respondents. However, fertilized eggs could have also originated from the Mekong River region much like the fermented fish products that have been attributed to the area (Ku 2013). Balut-eating most likely became established for its ease in portability, providing a quick need for protein and other nutrient-rich benefits.

However it came about, even before Magellan set foot in 1521, the country now known as Philippines had already enjoyed a long history of maritime trading with countries like Arabia, Persia, and India via Indonesia, beginning from the second century BCE if not earlier (Garcia 1979:8–34; Jocano 1975b:135–158). There is evidence that China was a direct trading partner by the year 982 (Scott 1989), and this interaction which led to the existence of the many types of *pansit* (noodles), *siopao* (meat bun), and *lumpia* (eggroll) that have been indigenized to local tastes and regional ingredients (Fernandez and Alegre 1988:17; Fernandez 2003) may have also led to the introduction of balut.

By the time of Spanish arrival, the residents of the Philippine archipelago had traded and intermarried and traveled throughout the Southeast Asia region as well as beyond. The 300-plus years of Spanish rule via Mexico added dishes like *adobo, menudo, paella,* and *embotido* which are typically enjoyed in fiestas along with *lechon* (roasted pig) as well as imported cheeses such as *queso de bola*, a type of Edam cheese made especially for the Filipino palate (Fernandez 2003; Magat 2013).

Influenced by the foodways of the Malay, Chinese, Spanish, and American groups and most recently the Mediterranean and Arabic forces that have left their imprint upon the recipes and foods brought back by OFWs, the result is that Filipino food is a "gastronomic telling of Philippine history" (Fernandez 2005:7). A "fusion" cuisine before it was in vogue, Filipino foodways may lead some to accuse it as an "imitation" cuisine; that is, if one believes in the existence of "authentic" Asian gastronomy (Ku 2013).

Unlike other Southeast Asian nations like Laos, Burma, and Vietnam, where the cuisine was "developed and preserved in lavish imperial courts," Filipino cuisine was established not by royal households as there were none, but instead, "many culinary traditions originated in the homes of elite, landed families" with each household generating its own batch of specialties that are passed on to succeeding generations (Besa and Dorotan 2006:15). This explains why the best Filipino cooking is perceived by many Filipinos to come from those homes with a tradition of good cooking, not necessarily from restaurants (Besa and Dorotan 2006:5).

No matter the foreign origin of the dish, however, any food can become a "Filipino" dish once tamed. As Fernandez points out, there is no mistaking a dish as being Filipino food if it has been indigenized by the citrus fruit *calamansi*, or the ubiquitous fish sauce called *patis* that provides much of the underlying *umami* flavor of dishes (Fernandez 2003). Most Filipinos in the diaspora would agree that it is the *sawsawan*, or condiments made up of "a galaxy of flavor-adjusters" including *patis*, soy sauce, *suka* (vinegar), *bagoong* (fermented shrimp paste), or tart mangoes and tomatoes sliced up and served in a pool of any one of the fermented native vinegars that would constitute the dish to become "Filipino" (Fernandez 2003:64). The resulting sour–salty–sweet and sometimes bitter notes in Filipino cuisine is at once familiar and unlike anything one has had before (Gold 2017), with hints of Pacific and Asian flavors at its core.

But rather than join in the battle waged in contemporary food fights between those who champion "authentic" cuisine over those who deliberately create and enjoy "bastardize" versions of that cuisine elsewhere other than the motherland, I wish to complicate this and emulate Robert Ji-Song Ku's call to examine the cultural politics of what makes a food "dubious" (2013:4). In the case of balut, unraveling its rise to prominence can shed light on the postmodern experiences of Filipinos and their transnational movements and how food can be used to promote identities, whether as a Filipino citizen in the diaspora, a savvy foodie with cultural capital in the United States, or any combination therein.

Online, the topic of Filipino food and identity seems to be a popular one, with varying but similar sentiments about a Filipino identity crisis. This manifests itself on the world stage with a lack of a signature Filipino dish that everyone can agree as "Filipino." Balut suffers no identity crisis; it is unmistakably itself, as "genuine" a food can get. Unlike adobo which can vary in taste with distinct vinegars and different meats, balut cannot be varied in its embryonic essence although it can be buried in pies and deep fried on a stick. Perhaps this is why it has become such a potent marker of Filipino ethnicity.

## "Ethnic" in America

In the United States, such immigrant food as balut has been classified as "ethnic food" because of its difference and subjected to questions of authenticity (Manalansan 2013:290). Asians in America and by extension, their foods, have been seen as "largely watered down" and "inauthentic" when compared to those in the imaginary homeland (Ku 2013:9). Enter balut in the picture, a visceral food that is unapologetically itself. No amount of pastry flour or seasoning can hide what it is. One either eats it or not. As such, it has become a potent identity marker for Filipinos and for non-Filipinos interested for various reasons, such as a tool to gain culinary capital.

My use of the word "ethnic" and "ethnicity" must be clarified at this point. Using the term "ethnic" continues the static categorization approach promulgated by the US census in accounting for the various groups in America, especially when it comes to Asian Americans (Zhang 2015:499–452). Zhang notes that sticking to an ethnic-based analysis of groups ignores the flexibility and transformative aspects of identity-making. Indeed, as pointed out earlier, there are many identities for the individual and the group (Dundes 1983). In order to analyze such an emerging practice as balut consumption in social media and in other, non-traditional contexts by Filipinos and non-Filipinos alike, new terms are needed. The use of "folkloric identity" defines the actual lore or folklore that is being practiced which assists in the creation of a group's identity (Zhang 2015). "Folkloric identity" would allow for a clearer picture of what is currently occurring in various heritage events and in private homes, as the practice of eating balut is no longer contained within the group that it was historically associated.

The consideration of folklore-in-practice moves away from the artificial binary of ethnic implied as "the Other" (Said 1978). Other scholars such as Krishnendu Ray further elaborate on the meaning of the term "ethnic," stating it is "a proximate but subordinate other, too close to be foreign, too different to be the self"(Ray 2016:1). Ray further accuses "theoretical sophisticates" of using the term as "an unutterable referent to color and inferiority, which is mostly covered over in pragmatic silence" (Ray 2016:4). However, Ray admits it remains a useful term to illustrate remaining differences between what is considered the Western normal and what is the assumed Other(s) (Ray 2016:4). I agree with his statement, as careful use of the word "ethnic" can bring awareness to gaps in representation. This work hopefully continues to illustrate such inequalities and brings to light, like Ray's work on the ethnic restaurateur (2016), other voices not always heard, namely, those from Filipino American immigrants or of Filipino heritage who are now involved in the collective formation of Filipino identities elsewhere in the diaspora.

## Making balut the traditional way

In the Tagalog language, the Filipino dialect chosen to be the national language of the Philippines, the word "*balutin*" means to encase, to wrap, or to envelope something. The name "balut" may have been etymologically derived from the word "*balutin*," as the traditional way of making the delicacy is to cover the eggs with sacks filled with rice husks that have been heated until hot. Only fertilized duck eggs with thick unbroken shells would be selected to become balut. Once chosen, these eggs would sit in the sun for several hours to remove the extra moisture before they are incubated in woven bamboo incubators or in bags of abaca hemp (Magat 2002; Maness 1950).

After a week, the eggs are "candled" or checked with a *silawan*, a box with a lightbulb that has a hole to hold the egg so the light can shine through the shell. If dark with veins, that means an embryo has formed and is developing. If there is nothing but a yolk, then the egg is infertile. Eggs that have cracked or where the embryo does not develop are made into *penoy*, a hard-boiled duck egg with a little or no apparent embryo that are eaten like balut.

These failed balut eggs or *penoy* are also widely consumed in the Philippines and consist of four types: *sariwang penoy* which resembles a fresh, regular egg; *higop* (literally to slurp or drink) which is *penoy* with a soup to drink; *penoy tuyo* (dry) where the reddish yolk is mixed with the white albumen and can be eaten with a spoon; and PSB or *penoy sa balut* which already has a very small embryo. Even spoiled balut where water has permeated the membrane of the egg are utilized despite its strong sulfur smell. These eggs are beaten and fried or used to top sweet rice cakes called *bibingkang abnoy* or *bibingkang itlog* (Fernandez 1996b:10).

One of my interviewees, J.J., described the "rotten eggs" prepared by her mother as omelets which she recalled as delicious and served with vinegar and garlic. As for the infertile eggs, these were made into salted duck eggs (*itlog na maalat*) by coating them with salted clay or soaking them in salted water before dying them red.

Also related to balut are the day-old male chicks that have been rejected by poultry farms which only selects females. These male chicks called "super-chicks" and "Day-O" are fried whole as *pulutan* (snacks) and sold in the streets and drinking places (Fernandez 1994:11).

Filipino foodways is characterized by a nose-to-tail, sustainable approach long before it came into fashion in the United States. Nothing goes to waste, and this illustrates the ethos of utilizing everything available, even "spoiled" eggs or unwanted male chicks. Filipinos learn to make do with what is around them due to the fact that many live in poverty (Claudio 1994:6).

Popular street foods besides balut demonstrate this ethos. The feet of chickens are barbequed and called "Adidas," roosters' combs are grilled and sold as "helmets," and chicken intestines are labeled "IUD" for its appearance (Fernandez 1994:10). Once known as the sleeping tiger of Asia, the Philippine economy soured under the Marcos dictatorship. While Imelda Marcos shopped for thousands of shoes, many a Filipino had to contend with eating whatever was available and affordable, such as chicken necks and pigs' ears, replacing chicken breasts, thighs, and pork that were once plentiful as street food (Fernandez 1994:9).

Balut consumption in the United States, where alternative sources of protein abound, must be understood within the context of Asian American immigration, which informed Filipino cultural practices and influenced food choices. Examining the balut production and distribution in the United States can illustrate how balut is made available to Filipinos and other Asian Americans.

## Balut-making in the United States

One sunny, early morning in January 2016, I drove down to Metzer Farms in Gonzales, California, about 2.5 hours south of San Francisco. I had first visited Metzer Farms two decades ago. The farm is still run by John Metzer who is now joined by his son, 29-year-old Marc. Metzer Farms sells about 350,000 eggs a year, although its main focus is to sell ducks. It produces about 2,000–4,000 balut a week as a side business, selling about 50 percent of the balut in the San Francisco Bay Area. With the assistance of two distributors, Metzer Farms sells balut in stores and in farmer's markets but also ships to other states. In addition, thanks to word-of-mouth, people can pick up balut directly from the farm. The farm sells salted eggs and *penoy*, in addition to balut.

John Metzer is a distinguished-looking man whose secret to a younger-looking skin is a healthy lifestyle that includes eating two duck eggs a day. Besides Marc, he and his wife Sharon have two children: 33-year-old daughter Janelle and Erin, 25.

John began his farm in 1978 with the intention of selling balut. While he was in his junior year at University of California at Davis studying animal science, John recalled how a man came to visit his father, who was raising ducks at the time as a hobby. The man wanted to buy at least 10,000 balut. So for the first 8–10 years of Metzer Farms, John focused exclusively on balut before he shifted his business to its current specialty of a waterfowl hatchery. One reason why John lessened his production of duck balut is the expense. Although making balut is relatively a cheap process, it is more profitable to hatch out the eggs to sell as ducklings instead of selling them unhatched as balut. It may well be that balut will once again become the main business instead of a sideline, as John shares that his son is looking to expand balut production.

During my latest visit to the farm, I noted its idyllic setting where young ducks cleaned and preened themselves in wide open, grassy areas separated by age (Figure 4). John explains that adolescent ducks which are not laying eggs yet are placed outside during the day, as he feels they do better out in the open air. The young ducks get a chance to be outside on the grass, mingling with others their age. When I asked John if the ducks had a pond to swim in, he explained that water is recreational to them. "The ducks don't need swimming water, they want it," John says. "It's a common misconception that they have to

**Figure 4** Adolescent ducks pastured at Metzer Farms.

have swimming water. They like it, they probably stay cleaner and prettier in it, but they don't have to have it 24/7."

The runoff from the water is a problem, as the ducks are a "little messier" than chickens, because their droppings are wetter. John describes the mess they make with water:

> With chickens, water is a nutrient. They drink it and walk away. With ducks, it's something for them to play in. And they splash it. And it gets into the dirt and becomes mud … they play in the mud and carry that around. So they can make a mess.

Besides the ducks pastured in the field, there were about 1,800 to 2,000 ducks in a building where they had plenty of room to move around with wooden shavings on the ground. The ground is cleaned regularly and fresh shavings are added twice a week (Figure 5).

Metzer Farms uses new technology to make balut. Up to 10 years ago, eggs would still be rotated as older eggs would generate more heat which would be utilized by the younger eggs. Since Metzer Farms began using single-stage incubators, the eggs are started at the same time and all eggs in an incubator are the same age. The eight incubators keep the eggs in a perfect temperature so that the eggs continue to develop (Figure 6).

**Figure 5** Ducks inside Metzer Farms.

**Figure 6** Incubator at Metzer Farms.

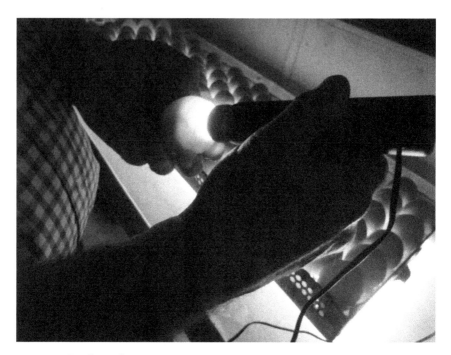

**Figure 7** Candling of egg at Metzer Farms.

All the eggs start at the temperature of 100.4, and every day the temperature is adjusted along with the increase in carbon dioxide. Higher levels of $CO_2$ make healthier ducks, John has found. He theorizes that the ducks' cardiovascular system seems to develop better with higher levels of $CO_2$.

Each incubator is affiliated with a profile which ensures the eggs remain at their best. Every two hours, the duck eggs are turned over automatically. Incubators can hold 22,000 eggs, with some incubators carrying up to 32,000 eggs. The incubators are heated with hot water and cooled with cold water. Eggs intended for balut production are candled twice, that is, these are lit by a special light at eight or nine days, and again at 17 days before they come out (Figure 7).

The process of making balut may have changed with the highly efficient incubators, but the way the egg develops into balut has remained constant. John describes the process of growth that occurs once an egg is fertilized:

> An egg that is fertilized … as soon as it is fertilized in the egg, it starts to grow. It's not as if it's laying one cell or two cells. There's thousands of cells by the time it's laid because it started to reproduce … But when that egg is laid, there is already very rudimentary beginnings of an embryo there … A lot

of people think it's just a single cell or it's capable of growing. No, as soon as that sperm penetrated that egg, that single cell, it started to grow and that's way up in the fallopian tubes. As it came down and the white was put around it and the shell was put around it, it's growing, the whole way.

Once an egg is laid, it cools down in nature. At the farm, John's employees put the eggs in a cooler where growth stops. When they put fertilized eggs back in an incubator, then these eggs will begin to grow again.

When asked about the reactions of people to the partially developed chick in a balut egg, John shakes his head at the remarks he has heard:

> Some people say, "Oh wow, it's an embryo, there's something there." Well you can say that of any fertile egg in the store, because they do sell fertile eggs in the store. There's a very small embryo in there. It's very small, but it has started to grow.

Fertilized eggs are perceived more nutritious than non-fertilized eggs, but they are not, according to John. "The only thing that is different between infertile and fertile eggs is that a fertile egg has sperm in there," laughs John. "And that's highly valuable."

Duck eggs, however, are more nutritious than chicken eggs. He cites a USDA analysis that reveals for every 100 grams of duck eggs, compared to 100 grams of chicken eggs, duck eggs have more vitamins and minerals. "They have more fat and more cholesterol, so they have more of everything than chicken eggs on average," John explains. "A fresh duck egg is more nutritious per gram, per ounce than a fresh chicken egg." For example, fertilized eggs are higher in calcium than regular eggs (Simoons 1991:365). Folk belief confirms the scientific evidence, as balut is especially encouraged for pregnant women and children to help with bone development.

**Table 1** Nutritional breakdown of balut

Embryonated duck egg—188 calories, 13.7 grams of protein, 14.2 grams of fat, 116 milligrams of calcium, 176 milligrams of phosphorous, 2.1 milligrams of iron, 875 micrograms of retinol, 435 micrograms of B-carotene equivalent, .12 milligrams of thiamine, .25 milligrams of riboflavin, 0.8 milligrams of niacin, and 3 milligrams of ascorbic acid

Source: W. Leung et al., *Food Composition Table for Use in East Asia* (Rome: FAO, 1972).

During a typical production cycle for ducks, which is about 40 weeks or 280 days, a duck would lay 100–223 eggs, depending on the breed. A duck's average life span is five to eight years. John estimates that at their peak, nine eggs would be produced by every 10 female ducks before gradually dropping down to five eggs a day. At that point, the ducks are no longer producing as much and this is borne out by the increasingly narrow pelvic bones that could be felt in the female ducks.

Because most of the breeds carried by the farm were chosen for their color and size, and not for their capacity to lay eggs, the ducks are not the most productive egg-laying birds. However, the two breeds which are the top layers in the farm are the White Layer and Golden 300 Hybrid ducks. Other breeds in the farm include Rouen ducks which have the greatest difference between the male and female ducks in coloring, and the Peking duck, a white breed where males and females are the same color but are sized differently. No matter what breed, however, all the ducks in the farm originated hundreds of years ago from wild mallard ducks and because of this, one can determine their sex by their voice.

Although some 20 years ago, Metzer Farms carried Muscovy ducks, which some believed to produce the best balut, the farm no longer keeps this breed. Muscovy ducks are genetically different from other ducks, and if John bred these with his other breeds, the resulting progeny would be infertile. "If you cross a horse and a donkey, you get a mule and a mule cannot reproduce as it is genetically different," John notes. "The same for Muscovy ducks if crossed with other ducks; it would be a mule duck."

John shares that when balut is sold, the customer does not ask what breed of duck produced it. Other factors such as shell color or size are requested, but not a specific breed. The farm's two distributors of balut prefer eggs that are large and some that are small, and the prices of balut depend on the weight of the egg. Eggs ordered from the farm's website ranges from pee wee size priced at 75 cents to jumbo-sized eggs at $1 a piece.

The farm's practice is to ensure that the young ducks get plenty of time outside on the grass. Ducks out on the grass are about four weeks old, and by seven weeks old, they are fully feathered. As soon as they get a full set of feathers, they will molt those out for another set of feathers. John shares that one of the interesting facts about raising ducks is there is an art even to the collection of their feathers and how these are separated.

John describes how the most valuable feathers are the down feathers, while the heavy wing feathers are the least valuable. When feathers are processed, they are washed and dried. Down feathers are separated from heavier feathers by a fan blowing straight up in front of shelves. "The higher the feathers blow up, the more valuable they are," he states. "The lighter feathers fall on the upper shelves while the heavier feathers do not get far from the fan. There's different levels of quality of feathers. It's pretty simple but that's still how they separate the feathers."

Metzer Farm's ducks have become famous and were regularly featured in the television show *Modern Family*. The Aflac ducks were also from the farm, when the insurance company's commercials would show a real live duck. Now the ducks used on the popular commercials are computer generated.

## From the farm to the market

Besides its ducks, what the farm has become famous for is the quality of its balut. Metzer Farms' balut is definitely fresh, agreed Arme Nicolas, who distributes Metzer Farms' eggs in two farmer's markets in northern California, in Fremont and Union City for the past 10 years. She has been selling farm fresh eggs for over 20 years at these two locations, which are sponsored by the Pacific Coast Farmer's Market Association.

In February 2016, I visited her at the Fremont farmer's market and in July 2016, I conducted participant observation fieldwork at the Union City market. Arme is of Filipino heritage with soft brown eyes and a ready smile. She supplies her customers with duck and chicken balut, fresh duck eggs, salted eggs, quail, and chicken eggs. Spring is the start of the busiest time for her and summer is even more hectic, while winter is the slowest. The reason is because of the weather; consumers come out when the weather is warmer and it is also the season for fresh Asian vegetables.

Her customers are people of various ethnicities but many of them are from the Filipino communities from Union City, Daly City, Vallejo, and San Jose, where there is a high demand for duck balut, salted eggs, and *penoy* which Arme describes as "incomplete fertilization."

When asked if she eats balut herself, Arme admits she does. "I drink the soup, eat the yolk and the albumen part but not the embryo. I give that to my husband," she says.

The first time Arme tasted balut was in the 1950s, as a child. Her parents wanted her to eat balut as it was a ready source of cheap protein. She describes the wide availability of balut in the Philippines:

> Everybody eats balut in the Philippines, my parents told me that these type of eggs are very rich in protein. If you live in the Philippines, it's very expensive to eat steak, pork or chicken meat. Only the rich can afford these luxurious meals, so as an alternative, duck balut is very affordable and nutritious.

In the beginning, she did not like eating balut. "At first, I didn't, because I was afraid of the embryo," recalls Arme. "It took me a while to get used to it but once you do, it's so tender." Arme prefers to eat balut that have developed enough but not to the point where there are discernable feathers or if it is too big. "If it's too big, then we have issues," she declares.

Arme confirms that the perfect balut is known as "*balut sa puti*" (where the embryo is wrapped in white albumen) and the incubation period is exactly 17 days. This kind of balut is preferred by Filipino American customers, while others such as the Vietnamese American customers prefer the eggs to be around 20 days old.

"The Vietnamese community like it when it's big," says Arme. "They want balut with hair. But not the Filipinos; the Filipinos like it small." Arme's customers include people of Vietnamese, Cambodian, and Chinese heritage who also eat balut, including others of different ethnicities who have lived in the Philippines and were exposed to the cultural consumption of fertilized eggs.

According to Arme, she has helped increase the sales of Metzer Farms' eggs, and through the years, the demand for balut has grown. Arme has sometimes ordered balut from Metzer Farms but the farm was not able to fulfill the order as the demand for hatched eggs outstripped the supply. "I tell the customers that it has to be pre-ordered ahead of time," she remarks.

Arme does not think that the increase in popularity has anything to do with balut being featured in reality television. "No, people know about it. They know what it's like … You have to have an acquired taste to eat balut," she emphasizes.

Marketing balut to curiosity seekers is something that Arme has done over the years. She considers herself as educating others about the cultural practice of eating balut:

> We market it to the curious ones. Because we have signs, in our stalls, that tell customers these are the eggs and there's a description. They ask what is balut, what is penoy. So we explain it to them, we educate them … The customer would say, "Oh let me try one of each." We even describe to them how it's eaten.

Arme also sells cooked balut and has salt available for those customers who want to eat it right at the spot. Besides salt, balut is eaten with pepper, *calamansi* (citric fruit) juice, lemon juice, tabasco, or vinegar.

There are other places that sell balut, such as flea markets, but these probably tend to not have fresh balut like in farmers' markets, according to Arme. She states that the price may be cheaper since these customers are "bargain hunters." Arme notes the freshness of the balut is of high-end quality at the farmer's markets.

Discussing her theory on how the practice of eating balut first started, Arme says the following:

> I believe it started way back in the early years in the province; they didn't have anything else to eat. They just boil those eggs, not knowing what it was. Because the ducks were just sitting on them until they hatched. The duck owners thought it was fresh duck eggs so when they boiled them, they were under the impression that it was fresh duck eggs which in fact they already had embryos in them. After boiling these eggs, people tasted them and concluded that it sure was edible and delicious. These are an excellent source of protein, so for those people that are lacking sleep or anemic, after eating balut they regain energy. Definitely the best source of protein instead of red meat.

Learning to eat balut requires the right cultural context. Arme understands why some may react against it, because balut is new to them.

> It might be gross for those people who haven't seen it, because of the features. There's the white part, the black part which is the head, and the feathers and all of that. And people would say, "Oh my goodness, she's eating gross stuff." It has to be acquired taste. You have to grow up with it. If you are a foreigner going into a country and you see people eating that, you would think they are gross people, that they are cannibals.

Arme is familiar with folklore featuring balut, especially the belief that it can act as an aphrodisiac.

> Men eat it because they say it makes their bones strong. It's a very common belief that when you eat balut, it makes your bones really, really strong and you will be up all night. Do you know what else they say about it? They are saying that balut is the Filipino version of Viagra.

That balut is a natural Viagra for men is something that Arme believes in, and she does not shy away from letting customers know.

> That's what we tell our people at the farmers' market. They laugh, and they go, "Oh, let me try one of those things." I get a kick out of that. They get more interested. "Really? So what's in there?" They don't have to take medicine anymore; it's natural.

According to Arme, some customers who try balut for its stimulating effects come back and let her know that it did work.

> We have customers especially the foreigners, that have not heard of it before or seen it before, but they heard it from their coworkers. Even the farmer's market managers, we initiate them to eat the balut. We dare them, so they know exactly what we are talking about and they can share that with other consumers at the farmer's market.

Those customers who have been initiated into eating balut praise the taste of the delicacy, says Arme.

> They say "oh my goodness, that thing I bought from you is really good. The only thing I don't like is the embryo." They like the yolk, they like the soup, and they like the albumen also known as the white portion of the balut.

Arme's Vietnamese American customers eat a variety of balut, including duck and chicken balut. Depending on the egg, raw or cooked balut price ranges from $1.50 to $1.75. Balut that are sold in flats are discounted; thus, regular balut customers receive a price break. They even call Arme to reserve their orders, especially if these balut have to travel to other cities and countries.

During the busy spring and summer seasons, Arme can sell approximately 1,000 eggs in both farmer's markets.

At the Saturday's market in Union City, the hours of operation are from 9 am to 1 pm but customers buy cooked balut as early as 7 am. On Sundays in the

Fremont market, the hours of operation are from 9 am to 2 pm but shoppers are already waiting for her arrival at 8 am to ensure they get the freshly cooked duck balut. The availability of balut declines during winter as the ducks go through the molting season. "The ducks don't lay as much, as a result the balut consumption is reduced by sixty percent," Arme notes. She considers it more exciting to sell balut around spring and summer.

## Balut's growing reputation

Metzer Farms' eggs are also sold in other places besides farmer's markets. The San Jose Flea Market, a local institution since 1960, sells balut among other things like produce, electronics, and all sorts of collectible items. I arranged to meet one of Metzer Farm's customers, Cayetano Araujo, who owns Cayetano Produce stall at the San Jose Flea Market. I had heard about Cayetano, who is of Mexican heritage, from Leo Cisneros, the manager of Metzer Farms.

Leo had mentioned to me that balut was now being sold at a flea market to Mexican Americans as well as Asian Americans. On March 11, 2017, I got together with Leo at the San Jose Flea Market and we walked to Cayetano's stall.

While discussing the market for balut, Leo notes that it has come a long way. "That's how far along balut has come, not only Asians but everybody's enjoying it. I know in the past, people have hesitated to try it," Leo says. "Balut has taken over. We have so much in demand. Even though it is cold season now and ducks are not laying the eggs as much, the demand's still there."

When we arrived at Cayetano Produce, Leo agrees to also be my interpreter, as I do not speak fluent Spanish. Leo has supplied Cayetano Produce with balut for about nine years. Cayetano Produce sells dried fruit, nuts, and sweets (Figure 8). Its owner, Cayetano Araujo, has sold balut for the last 23 years on the weekends and estimates that during the height of the balut consumption before the Great Recession, he would sell about an average of 1,000 balut per weekend.

The downturn in the economy has affected the balut sales, as people tend to cut down on expenses. "You can't afford treats, it's a snack," Cayetano points out. These days, during the slow time in winter, he will sell about 100–200 balut on a weekend. During the summer, Cayetano sells more.

**Figure 8** Cayetano Araujo being interviewed by author and Leo Cisneros at San Jose Flea Market.

The cost is $1.10 per large balut egg. Each weekend morning, he cooks the balut early and brings them hot to the stall, serving them with vinegar and chile powder (Figure 9).

When I asked him if balut has any health benefits, Cayetano answers in the affirmative. He himself has tried balut, and he described feeling energetic after eating it. One balut and two beers can give one a lot of stamina, says Cayetano with a laugh.

Speaking mostly in Spanish, Cayetano lists the benefits of eating balut. "*Si, bueno per energia, y la cabeza … muchas benefias*" (trans. "Yes, good for energy, and the head … much benefits"). Cayetano emphasizes that people should know the benefits of balut, to give it a chance, and try it more for its benefits. He sees more Latinos eating balut now because of the benefits and it is healthy for them. "It gives energy, helps with headaches and migraines and tastes like chicken soup," he states.

In his everyday practice, Cayetano tries to educate his customers, encouraging them to try the balut, as it might help them with either their headache or energy.

**Figure 9** Balut and condiments served at the stall.

Both he and Leo believe that the key is to educate people about the medicinal and health benefits to balut. It is understandable if some people are scared of trying balut. "They are scared of the unknown," admits Leo. Although Cayetano has not seen balut portrayed on television, he recalls that in the past, many people were asking for balut as they were familiar with it from watching the TV shows.

When Cayetano first took over the business from the previous owner who was a Filipino American, his clientele was mostly Filipinos and they would patronize his stall for balut. Later on, Cayetano's customers grew to include more Hispanic people and he started to tell them about the benefits of balut.

Although Cayetano has eaten balut, Leo has never tried balut himself, despite knowing about balut for 20 years. "The reason I have never tried balut is because I just haven't had a craving for it," he says. "It has crossed my mind, just to see what all the fuss is about. I might give them a try one day. For now I will continue taking pleasure on seeing people enjoy them."

Not knowing what it tastes like has not stopped Leo from taking balut to his Asian friends' parties and he is the most popular one there, as he arrives v the goods. But his Filipino friends give him a hard time. How can he stand by the product, but not eat it? He laughed at the question. "If I do eat it, I would start off with penoy," he affirms. "I've taken them to the parties and I've seen them eat it and enjoy it"(Figures 10–14).

**Figure 10**  Unshelled balut egg encased in its membrane—Courtesy of Albert Magat.

**Figure 11**  Overview of peeled balut—Courtesy of Albert Magat.

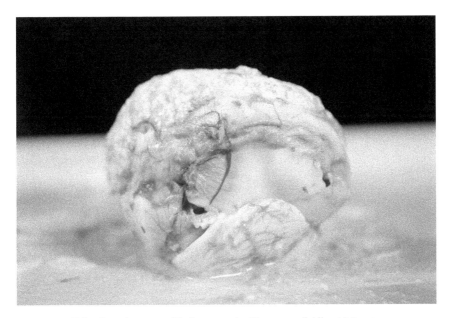

**Figure 12** Side view close-up of *balut sa puti*—Courtesy of Albert Magat.

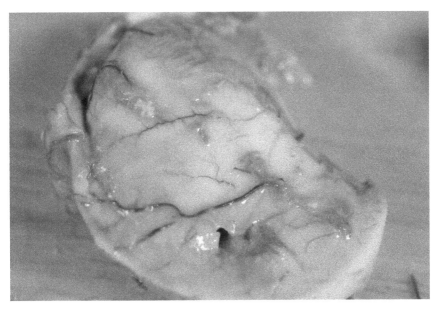

**Figure 13** Close-up of *balut sa puti* embryo encased in albumen—Courtesy of Albert Magat.

**Figure 14** A balut egg, deconstructed. From left to right, shell, membrane, embryo, and yolk. At foreground, more yolk—Courtesy of Albert Magat.

# 2

# A Nation in an Egg

On August 2, 2013, *Business Insider* which bills itself as the "largest business news site on the web," featured its host having a sit-down tutorial with the owner of a popular fine dining establishment in Manhattan called Maharlika.[1] Maharlika specializes in "authentic Filipino modern" cuisine and features balut on its menu. The resulting video was titled "We ate balut—the absolute strangest food you can find in New York."

During the tutorial, Maharlika owner Nicole Ponseca seemingly spears the neck of the partially developed duck and proffers the image to the camera, magnifying the effect. After the eating lesson, the *Business Insider* host returns to the office and offers balut to three colleagues who register different reactions. There are plenty of close-ups of the duck fetus and the subsequent 4,500-plus comments by viewers contained an abundance of disgusted remarks and expletive-filled judgments of what other people eat.

*Business Insider*'s marketing team must have recognized the polarizing reactions (read: more publicity) of its viewers and used that to leverage even more visibility for its website and for the restaurant Maharlika. Since that initial airing, the video is available not just on the *Business Insider*'s website but it is also uploaded to YouTube which registered over 800,000 views four years later. The website also created a Facebook page dedicated solely to the segment and more than 12 million viewers have watched it as of January 2019.

Among those who watched the video was an animal activist by the name of Gabrielle Hardy, who then created a petition to ban balut. Posting the petition on the website yousignanimals.com, Hardy was quoted as stating, "The truth is that this food is disgusting and should not be served in a restaurant. I am therefore asking the restaurant to get balut off the menu as soon as possible!" (Rappler 2015). The cofounder of the New York Animal Rights Allianc

America went one step further and labeled eating balut as "murder" (Tagala 2015).

In two weeks, the petition gathered close to its goal of 5,000 signatures. Other petitions to ban balut in countries like Australia and Great Britain have been initiated but none received the coverage that the New York petition did. An alleged counter petition by Filipino New Yorkers reputedly gathered more than 50,000 signatures at the same period (Pinoy 2015), but I was not able to confirm its veracity. But the petition authored by activist Hardy was given widespread publicity and was reported in several reputable news websites, including the major Philippine news outlet ABS-CBN.

News of the petition to force balut off the menu was greeted with disdain by many Filipino Americans. Leah Abraham of Boca Raton, Florida, was quoted as saying "It's not murder, not at all. I think it's disrespectful to us as Filipinos. I think they do that out of ignorance" (Tagala 2015).

The restaurant owner, Ponseca, went a step further, stating that "this isn't pro-balut or anti-balut. This is a choice to be pro-Filipino, which I am" (Tagala 2015). Ponseca compared the right to having balut as akin to the right to choose one's religious beliefs. She thanked the activist for "shedding light" on balut which was more popular than ever before. In the end, however, the petition seems to have been dropped. As of 2019, Maharlika's menu revealed that balut was still being served at $4 a pop.

Although activists such as Hardy may have intended the ban to be passed and balut to be removed from the menu, what transpired instead was more visibility for the restaurant Maharlika (Tagala 2015). Already, the restaurant did not lack for exposure. It had been featured favorably in the *New York Times* and the *New York Magazine* and the restaurants' owners had sponsored three years of balut-eating contests, along with its sister restaurant Jeepney. The contests had been covered in mainstream media ranging from the *Asian Journal* to NBC News. In 2014, *Ripley's Believe it or Not* wrote about the contest where the three-time champion, Filipino American Wayne Algenio, ate 40 balut eggs in five minutes.

The events surrounding the petition, along with the remarks emanating from the restaurant owner, activists, and the video that led to the ban as well as comments from well-respected Filipino American chefs which will be discussed below, raise issues concerning nationalism, culinary nationalism as well as the question of authenticity which continue to resonate in food studies. Also apparent in the discourse is the competing identity politics which surround the topic of balut consumption. Tensions are apparent between the way balut-eating has been marketed by Filipino Americans and how it is portrayed as a strange, "weird" food in Western traditional and social media. Such disjunctions between identity politics and nationalist sentiments define the concept of gastronationalism (DeSoucey 2010).

The reactions of many Filipino Americans express a form of culinary nationalism which has assisted the arrival of Filipino cuisine in the US. Culinary nationalism or the use of food to construct national identity is "alive and well," in spite of (or I submit because of) travel, technology, and the media (Ferguson 2010:105).

The culinary nationalism that is also being exhibited by Filipino Americans is in part a reaction to the legacy of colonial rule beneath Spanish and American powers which had impacted the perception of Filipino foodways both in the Philippines and in America, contributing to how balut has been perceived and continues to be seen.

Eating can already be political (see, e.g., Long 2015; Pollan 2006). In choosing to eat balut, I suggest that many Filipinos reaffirm nationalist sentiments and strengthen a collective identity with other Filipinos throughout the world (De Soucey 2010:448). The boundaries between the insiders and the outsiders of the culture are made clearer, with balut helping to delineate an "imagined community" (Anderson [1983] 1991).

## Balut and Filipino foodways

As mentioned previously, balut has been enjoyed as a delicacy for centuries, at least since 1834 if not earlier (Roberts 1837:60–61). Since then, balut has been eaten by Filipinos everywhere not just for nutrition but also to mark imagined ties to the motherland (Anderson [1983] 1991). In the United States, the marketing of balut by restaurants such as Jeepney and Maharlika, both top eateries on the vanguard of the new Filipino modern cuisine, plays with the nationalist tendencies of Filipino migrants and the desire of others to consume the exotic popularized by contemporary foodie discourse (Heldke 2003). Balu served in Filipino restaurants is not new, as it has been previously found in low-price *turo-turo* restaurants where the food is kept warm in covered trays. But fine dining restaurants focusing on Filipino food are relatively recent and so is the featured item of balut on those menus. The fact that a street food is included in the menu of an upscale restaurant like Maharlika is a direct result of its exposure in reality television and travel shows which have further stoked people's appetites to indulge in culinary tourism (Long 2004). As such, balut's presence in this particular moment of American food history can reveal the current politics of identity and social milieu experienced by Filipino Americans.

Food as an avenue to express a nation's culture and collective identities have been written about (see, e.g., Appadurai 1988; Ferguson 2010; Ku 2013; Pilcher 1998). However, studies on Filipino foodways and its linkages to Filipino identity have been sparse, with the exception of several valuable articles appearing in a collection of Asian American food studies in 2013 (Mabalon 2013; Manalansan 2013; Orquiza 2013).

The pioneer scholar in Filipino food studies is Doreen Fernandez, who tackled the Philippines's complex history of colonialism and trading along with geographical factors which have influenced its foodways (1994; Fernandez and Alegre 1988). Describing Filipino food as "a gastronomic telling of Philippine history" (Fernandez 2005:7), Fernandez also noted that it is regionalization that marks Filipino cuisine and that if there is one national dish, it would be *sinigang*, a sour stew that can be flavored with a variety of available citrus fruits, including tamarind or guava.

The sour component in indigenous cuisine was present by the time the Spanish arrived in the Philippines in the sixteenth century, with the use of vinegar by native people already in place. It may well have led the Spanish to use the term "*adobo*" to describe a dish that resembles their own recipes which featured meat simmered with wine and spices (Magat 2015). Although *adobo* is the front runner for the national dish, a singular version of it does not exist as the way it is made depends on the region where the cook originates. Adobo can be prepared various ways with different meats, with or without coconut milk, with or without soy sauce. Although techniques and ingredients may vary, however, it is unmistakably *adobo* if a meat or seafood or chicken is cooked in vinegar, garlic, and soy sauce (or not) with spices like peppercorn and bay leaves. This pickling technique in vinegar is also similar to Mexican *adobado* dishes, but in general there is no use of chilies in Filipino *adobo* unless it is from the southern areas of the Philippines.

Showcasing the versatility of adobo, Filipino chef Charles Olalia of the tiny, acclaimed casual restaurant Rice Bar in Los Angeles, prepared a different *adobo* dish each week for a whole year. This was a feat breathlessly reported about in the *Los Angeles Times*. Olalia described *adobo* as "very versatile, but there are certain notes that you need to hit; it can skew Japanese, Singaporean, Chinese, but you are definitely eating something from the Philippines" (Scattergood 2017). Main spices are hard to pin down for Filipino cuisine, with the element of sourness an important factor which has proven difficult to describe for many a food writer. This lack of a national dish and a hard-to-define spice profile may add to the reasons why Filipino food has not been as popular until recently as other Asian cuisines.

Which is why balut and its simplicity may have been a reason it has been catapulted as a symbolic marker of national identity, capturing the imagination of Filipinos (and others) in the United States and elsewhere who want to try and eat it, whether online or in festivals. There is basically only one way to eat it (although it can be deep fried or put in dough). The fertilized egg is so intrinsically related to the Philippine landscape that even when eaten out of the borders of the Philippine nation, it creates an imagined community for the eater (Anderson [1983] 1991). Its portability is an advantage, its ability to challenge the consumer is a benefit to separate those who do not want to be identified as "Filipino." It has been remarked elsewhere that balut is a liminal food (Matejowsky 2013; also see Turner 1967). I would like to expand this insight to offer a nuanced interpretation of liminality.

Taking off from Matejowsky's application of folklorist Arnold Van Gennep's rite-of-passage to balut consumption (Matejowsky 2013; Van Gennep [1909] 1965), I see balut consumption in specific contexts as fitting more of what Turner noted as a "liminoid" phenomenon where a sense of play is apparent (Turner 1974). The expression of identities that arises in these moments "of play, fun, even commerce" (Abrahams 2003:213) when balut is being consumed in certain circumstances whether involving OFWs returning from abroad, or Americans intent in filming themselves eating it for their vlogs, is what I am concerned with here.

In the case of overseas workers or Filipino migrants, they are physically separated from the motherland. They can be seen in a transitional or liminal state in their day-to-day lives far from home, but once they have an opportunity to eat balut, they can be incorporated into the imagined community of Filipinos via the ingestion of a national food which has the ability to provide homesick consumers a temporary feeling of belonging or citizenship. Arjun Appadurai coined the term "community of sentiment" (Appadurai [1990] 1996:8) and this aptly describes how the diasporic Filipino community scattered around the world are held together by the sentiments emanating from print capitalism (Anderson [1983] 1991), social media as well as the practice of Filipino expressive culture no matter where Filipinos are located. This includes events as big as the observation of the Philippine Independence Day throughout the Filipino diaspora as well as the small, everyday consumption of a food such as balut which requires a certain amount of effort to prepare and procure, like other Filipino foods that are longed for by those who are far from home. Such a practice as eating balut can help create a sense of locality for those able to maintain their native dietary habits.

Balut has an entire foodways that is built around a fertilized egg's transformative shifts in flavor and quality. "Whoever discovered balut stumbled onto the fact that food has changing excellences (taste, texture) as it evolves and develops," writes Fernandez. "Thus between the egg and the full-grown duck, there are stages that bear exploring—and eating" (Fernandez 1996b:10). This flexibility is a hallmark of Filipino foodways which uses available resources in a sustainable manner, utilizing everything nose-to-tail, something that has become fashionable again in haute cuisine discourse (for more on Filipino food consumption, see Alegre and Fernandez 1988:17; Fernandez 1996a, b).

The culture of balut is still alive and well in the Philippines, with various stages of embryonic eggs being consumed by people as well as balut with yolk that has been compromised or "rotten" being enjoyed in omelets and on top of sweets as pointed out in Chapter 1. Although it is not of the same stature as high-status foods like caviar or foie gras, balut's production is now being legislated in the Philippines and taken seriously (Reyes-Estrope 2017). The consumption of the embryonic duck egg is arguably as controversial and politicized as foie gras, with the right to eat balut anywhere becoming an important way for some Filipino Americans to defend their culture.

For the last two decades, balut has become more and more a marker of identity for Filipino Americans, the second biggest Asian American group in the United States (US Census 2012). As I noted earlier, the Philippines sends about 1 out of 10 of its citizens to work abroad, making the country the third largest remittance sender in the world, behind India and China (Asis 2017). Balut's symbolic resonance is felt elsewhere in the Filipino diaspora, as will be shown below. Discussions about balut consumption in the Filipino diaspora are significant because the practice of "Filipinoness" is informed by the experiences of other Filipinos in multiple sights and locations. "Identifications with other peripheral and racialized spaces within and without the U.S. national borders form and inform Filipino/Filipino American identity" which situate Filipino Americans globally (Isaac 2006:xxv).

Although balut is a popular street food in Philippines, not everyone eats it and there are class distinctions that govern its consumption (Magat 2002). Moreover, there are distinct variances between balut consumption in the Philippines and in the Filipino diaspora. Balut consumption in the United States by those of Filipino heritage is for enjoyment but also falls along the lines of culinary nationalism, whereas balut is eaten more for nutritional purposes in the Philippines.

In this chapter and throughout the rest of the book, I will look at questions including why would balut be the chosen symbol to construct national identity versus other, more widely consumed dishes such as adobo? How did such a food, traditionally a low-key, insider food along with dishes such as *dinuguan* (meat stew made of pig's blood and intestines) become the most visible Filipino dish as seen in social media and mainstream American television? What makes balut a Filipino dish, with the power to "authenticate" the consumer as "Filipino" when the egg itself was produced in a California duck farm or in Prague or Sydney?

## Nationalism and the Philippine-American relationship

To understand how a food such as balut is being used to create a national identity (a fascinating example of culinary nationalism), an explorat of Filipino nationalism is required along with a short background of

Philippine-American historical relationship. What does Filipino nationalism mean for Filipino Americans? If a nation is indeed an "imagined political community" and nationalism is a "cultural artefact" that must be analyzed in terms of how it came into being, its meanings and why it can provoke "profound emotional legitimacy" (Anderson 1983:4–5), then it is necessary to reflect on the complicated historical relationship between the Philippines and the United States which continues to influence the experience of Filipino Americans. Much has been written on this topic (see, e.g., Karnow 1989's popular account; see Rafael 2000 and Shaw and Francia 2002 for a thoughtful analysis from Filipino/Filipino American scholars). I offer a short summary below.

I had noted in Chapter 1 that the United States had come into possession of the Philippines when it defeated Spain in 1898, in the Spanish-American war, while at the same time that a Philippine independence movement was being waged against the Spanish by revolutionary fathers such as Andres Bonifacio. Filipino nationalism can be understood as developing from colonization, that when Filipinos first began to imagine a nation, it constituted a revolutionary act, at least to the Spanish colonial officials (Rafael 2003). "Without colonialism, there would have been nothing to break from … Filipino nationalism strangely enough owes its emergence to the very thing it sought to reject. It is not too far-fetched to say that colonialism was the forebearer of nationalism in the Philippines" (Rafael 2002:362).

By February 1899, the Philippine-American war had begun and the United States took active steps to possess what it saw as its legitimate territory. But Filipino revolutionaries still harbored the dream of an independent country, which continued to drive them in engaging American troops in guerilla warfare. The official proclamation that the Philippine-American war had ended in 1902 did not account for the continuing mutinies that lasted for over a decade (Ileto 1979).

Writing about the term "amigo warfare" that the Americans used to label Filipino resistance, Filipino historian Reynaldo Ileto described the burning, looting, raping, and murders that occurred in towns such as Candelaria and Tiaong, where Filipinos resisted the American superior forces through various mechanisms, like feigning defeat, playing dead, shifting identities, allowing oneself to be flexible with the wind like the bamboo (Ileto 2002:7). The official toll of the war resulted in over 200,000 Filipinos dead, including civilians. The total number of American dead was estimated around 4,200. Yet the Philippine-American war is largely forgotten, even described as an "insurrection," which implies that Americans were putting down an illegitimate rebellion when the reality was that the United States was fighting Filipinos who wanted independence (Ileto 2002). A "lacuna" (Ileto 2002) exists about this historical event, understood as a "cultural aphasia" (Isaac 2006) regarding the history and aftereffects of American colonization, which has left Filipinos "Americanized without becoming Americans" (Karnow 1989:209). Is the forgetting due to the indebtedness or "utang ng loob" (lifelong debt) that Filipinos feel to the very people that caused the war to happen (Ileto 2002)?

Adding to the lifelong debt obligation is the fact that the Americans came to educate and reform the educational system of the Philippines. Along the way, the Philippine-American war was turned into a "non-event" and for generations, Filipinos who were educated by the American colonial system "did not see the war as the U.S. suppression of their cherished revolutionary and nationalist dreams" but rather a "misguided" and "even stupid, rejection of a gift of further enlightenment" (Ileto 2002:4).

The "forgetting" of the Philippine-American war may also be due to the prevailing image of the unique relationship that the two countries allegedly have, where kinship is alluded to with the use of terms such as "little brown brother" (Ileto 2002:3).

This complex relationship with America, both its colonizer and its benevolent benefactor, painted the experiences of the early Filipino Americans who were drawn to America. With the chaotic experience of war and the increased emphasis on crops benefiting American interests and usurping traditional ways of living, many Filipinos were disenfranchised from their land and they sought work. From 1906 to 1934, an estimated 175,000 Filipinos, who were now American nationals, immigrated to the United States to find work (Alegado 1992:158). Most of the early migrants were from agricultural provinces of Pangasinan and Ilocos Norte, farmers and residents who were uprooted from their land caused by the shift to manufacturing under American colonialism (Eviota 1992:64; Mabalon 2013:151).

## Filipino American migration

This first large wave of Filipino migrants was composed of mostly unmarried male Filipinos, with some Filipinas. Due to the declining numbers of Chinese and Japanese laborers in Hawai'i, Filipinos were recruited by the Hawai'i Sugar Planters and sent to work in sugar cane plantations between 1906 and 1910 (Reinecke 1996:1–2; Mariano ([1933] 1972:3). In California, they went to work in the fields as well as canneries, and in Alaska, they gutted fish and worked in the mines. Once in America, Filipinos continued to experience extreme hardships.

These Filipino migrant workers were known as "manongs" in California while in Hawai'i, they were called "sakadas." By 1920 in Los Angeles, there were Filipinos in the service sector working as janitors, porters, and houseboys. A smaller group were "fountain pen boys" (also known as "pensionados"), students sent by the American colonial system to attend college while working to support themselves in menial positions (Koerner 2007). They settled in the area that is known as Little Tokyo today, and they also headed to the suburbs of Los Angeles such as Carson and the South Bay. They congregated and sought refuge from homesickness in places like the Pearl Harbor Café and the Tumble-in-Café which operated in San Pedro, at the corner of Beacon and Sixth Streets in the 1920s (Ibanez and Ibanez 2009).

With the passage of the 1924 Immigration Act which restricted Chinese and Japanese immigration, thousands of Filipinos immigrated to Hawai'i and to California, many bypassing Hawai'i altogether to head to the Delta region in California (Mabalon and Reyes 2008:7). By the late 1920s, Filipinos "drove the economic engine of the region" in Stockton, making it the largest Filipino community outside the Philippines (Mabalon and Reyes 2008:7).

American society was not open to Filipinos, and so they formed their own mutual aid groups and associations (Koerner 2007:47). Filipino organizations were based on village or regional association such as the Pangasinan Association of Southern California which regularly met in the 1920s and 1930s (Ibanez and Ibanez 2009:15). Other associations were Filipino church groups and Filipino community associations. In Hawai'i where Filipinos celebrated their centennial anniversary in 2006, such events as Rizal Day cultivated the nationalism felt by Filipino sakadas and their families. Rizal Day was observed by a reenactment of Filipino hero Jose Rizal's final day before his execution complete with the recitation of his farewell poem to his motherland, "Mi Ultima Adios" as well as the election of a Rizal Day queen, dancing and feasting (Gonsalves and Labrado 2011:24–25).

Filipinos in America called themselves "Pinoy" (Filipino) and Pinay (Filipina) and were ostracized both politically and socially and had to confront overt racism that was exacerbated by legislation forbidding marriage with white women (Takaki 1989:330–331). They could not vote or buy land. The passing of the Tydings-McDuffie Act in 1934 resulted in Filipinos in America being reclassified not as American nationals, but as aliens. They continued to be exposed to tough working conditions and were stereotyped as being immune to the inhalation of peat dust or the pains resulting from the constant stooped labor during agricultural work (Melendy 1981:75).

As a survival tactic during the Depression, many Filipinos banded together and lived in one place to share living and food expenses as they were not eligible for the New Deal, eating whatever food they could glean from campos or canneries (Mabalon 2013:155–157). Pigs' necks, tails, and feet and fish heads were supplemented by wild vegetables and illegal hunting around the Delta. By 1930, Filipinos in America were portrayed in the media as having a squalid lifestyle with a "barbaric" standard of eating to match (Mabalon 2013:155).

Almost 100,000 Filipinos lived in California and Hawai'i by the time of the Second World War (Mabalon and Reyes 2008:7). In places like Stockton, they were forbidden to enter white spaces which brought up problems of housing and lack of places to congregate. Such signs as "No Dogs and No Filipinos Allowed" and "Positively No Filipinos Allowed" were common, for example (Mabalon and Reyes 2008:7).

Faced with such difficult conditions, Filipinos in America formed their own business and associations, establishing a community of Little Manila in downtown Stockton which consisted of six blocks near Chinatown. "Because the neighborhood drew thousands of Filipinos from all over the nation, Stockton's Little Manila became the heart of Filipino America" (Mabalon and Reyes 2008:7). Although Little Manila was mostly razed in the 1950s, it is now recognized for its important role in Filipino American history, thanks largely to the efforts of Filipina American historian Dawn Mabalon.

Stockton's Filipino Americans were critical in the establishment of labor organizations which advocated for workers' rights. Filipino American Larry Itliong was the leader of the 1965 Delano grape strike and it was he who urged Cesar Chavez to come and join Filipino strikers. This alliance helped form the United Farm Workers Organizing Committee (Mabalon and Reyes 2008:39).

After a day of working in the fields, Filipinos spiffed up in good-looking suits and sought respite and entertainment in taxi dance halls and pool halls. They spent a dime per dance of their hard-earned money to be able to dance with women (Parrenas 1998). Filipino men were known as "sharp dressers" who attracted white women and simmering tensions between Filipinos and white men often resulted in race riots (Burns 2013:61). Tailors and dry cleaning businesses were kept busy by their smartly dressed clientele. From the 1920s to the 1970s, other businesses run by Filipinos include "restaurants, grocery stores, churches, beauty salons, barber shops, pool halls ... These sites served multiple purposes" whether it acted as a social center or labor recruitment (Mabalon and Reyes 2008:47).

Filipinos in America sent photographs featuring themselves in formal suits or cowboy outfits, and these greeting cards depicted the American dream and further stimulated others back in the Philippines to come to the United States. "Life in America allowed immigrant Pinoys to play with different personas and identities" (Mabalon and Reyes 2008:21).

One of the most integral places in Little Manila was Lafayette Lunch Counter, which was owned by Mabalon's grandfather and was a critical hub for Filipinos such as writer Carlos Bulosan, whose classic *America Is in the Heart* chronicled the hardships of Filipino migrant life in the 1930s. The Lafayette Lunch Counter served three generations of Filipinos with adobo and diniguan and provided food to even those who could not afford to pay. Besides the Lafayette Lunch Counter, there were other restaurants in Stockton and they proliferated after the Second World War (Mabalon and Reyes 2008:57).

## The birth of Filipino American foodways

The Lafayette Lunch Counter in Stockton, the Pearl Harbor Café in 1920s San Pedro, and others like these eateries provided Filipino Americans a sense of cultural belonging along with fellow migrants. These early restaurants were casual diners, meant for insiders and not outsiders to the community. By providing dishes which relied on what was available, these pioneer diners helped form Filipino American cuisine. Dishes that were served in these restaurants already harbored traces of the mother country as well as the surrounding American environment. This results in the formation of expressive culture being different from the practices in the old country (Lockwood and Lockwood 1998:21). It was a cuisine that was marked with the limitations, restrictions, and working conditions that Filipino migrants were experiencing (Mabalon 2013).

"What Filipinas/Filipinos produced in the fields and canneries and cooked and ate in the decades before World War II was shaped by the brutality of industrialized agriculture, the grinding poverty of the Depression years, pitiful agricultural wages and conditions, anti-Filipina/o racist violence, exclusion and deportation, labor repression, and an extreme sex-ratio imbalance" (Mabalon 2013:148). In Alaska, for example, the Filipinos worked in salmon canneries from the 1910s to the 1970s and they improvised by making fish sauce from fermented salmon scraps instead of tiny shrimps or anchovies. They married Native Alaskan women who taught them to hunt moose, porcupine, geese, and ducks (Mabalon 2013:160). Adobo was made with seal and beaver meat and vegetables like wild peas were sought as "bukayong" (Mabalon 2013:160–161). Meanwhile, in places like Louisiana, Filipinos who settled in Saint Malo in the eighteenth to the early twentieth century caught shrimp and taught shrimp-drying techniques which continue to be used today. In the Delta region of California, near Stockton, they fished for salmon in the rivers which was an illegal act.

Filipino foodways in the United States owe much to these early migrant collective experiences. Thus, it can be said that Filipino American cuisine was marked by hunting and foraging for local foods while making due with what was available (Mabalon 2013:171). This is much in line with the sustainable ethos present in Filipino cuisine in the Philippines.

In addition to these conditions in their environment, the Filipino early migrants also bore the memory of the denigration of their native cuisine, as the American reformers back home had pushed for the consumption of We goods and dishes. I had previously noted that during the half centi colonization under the United States, American educational reform promoted the desire for Western goods such as canned meat, powdered milk, baked goods, and dishes marked by ease of preparation and with using modern technology. At the same time, the value of Filipino food with its emphasis on fresh fish, rice, and vegetables was devalued (Orquiza 2013). The American agenda was so successful that after the Second World War, American goods were even more desired, and Spam and corned beef were coveted (and continue to be favored) as status symbols (Fernandez 2002).

Such sites as the Lafayette Lunch Counter and numerous other unnamed Filipino eateries which have not been documented in photos or in archival collections may be theorized as the places that allowed for Filipino culinary nationalism to first flourish. When food is used to construct a national identity, culinary nationalism results (Ferguson 2010), and imagining the nation becomes more vivid and real with each dish that reminds one of home.

## Nation-building through the senses

The emotive power of culinary nationalism draws from a large dose of nostalgia, specifically culinary nostalgia (Mannur 2007). People who experience dislocation, such as Filipino migrants, whether through forced or voluntary migration, then turn to food to assist them in dealing with the separation from their homeland. Food anchors the displaced subject, while signaling her/his cultural difference (Mannur 2007:13).

This is demonstrated by balut's presence in countries where Filipinos are present, such as Greenland, United Arab Emirates (Ponce de Leon 2016) (although bringing balut into the country has since been banned due to health regulations), and Italy, to name a few places. Wherever there are Filipinos to be found, one will find balut. For example, during Sundays at the Termini Station in Rome, enterprising Filipinas on their day off from working as domestic helpers sell balut and other Filipino foods in plastic containers hidden inside designer bags. The piazza outside Termini Station is transformed to be a temporary space with the aid of foods such as balut, helping create a sense of home where one can relax and briefly restore the self (Magat 2003). The tastes of home, the sights, and smells of familiar foods like balut along with the sounds of other Filipina women speaking in familiar dialects enable a kind of homecoming which allow the migrant women to return to their imaginary nation. "Diasporic return occurs not only in the moment of physically setting foot on homeland soil, it also can be through emotion-filled and memory-ridden food events in the 'elsewhere'" (Manalansan 2013:292).

Food can mark a place and make a space (Jones 2005:134). In Hong Kong, a similar scene to Rome's Termini Station unfolds each Sunday magnified further with the presence of more than 100,000 Filipinas who turn Central Hong Kong into Little Manila. The olfactory and gustatory senses, coupled with the visual as well as the sense of touch, are powerful enough to reinforce a sense of Filipino-ness for Filipinas. It is here where food is used as a way to help Filipinas recover from "subtle forms of sensory reculturation" which is prevalent in their work as domestic workers in Hong Kong households (Law 2001:266). Eating Filipino foods "articulates national identity" that is not possible in the Philippines with the foods signifying Filipina identity in an affirmative light (Law 278). Whether one is in Rome or Hong Kong or elsewhere in the Filipino diaspora, eating Filipino foods such as balut is a way of ingesting the homeland.

Unlike other foods where preparation, ingredients, and location are essential for the food to become the ideal dish, the fertilized egg somehow communicates a landscape, much like the French ingredients in a pot au feu (see Ferguson 2010). Yet how does it do that when the egg itself is from elsewhere other than the Philippines? What happens when balut is consumed in the elsewhere? Unlike eating bouillabaisse in Marseille which can qualify the meal as quintessentially French (Ferguson 104), balut can be taken apart from the motherland and be eaten anywhere in the world but still retain its power to "authenticate" the eater to feel "Filipino" or obtain honorary citizenship via the act of eating it. This power comes from its ability to separate the "intrepid" eaters from the gawkers, the insiders from the outsiders. Foreigners who attempt to consume it can also gain acceptance and admiration, sometimes grudgingly, while mediating local politics (Matejowsky 2013).

If indeed, Filipino nationalism was born from a "moment of rupture" (Rafael 2002:362) when nationhood became envisioned by breaking away from Spanish colonialism, balut may be the perfect vehicle to carry the natio' identity via culinary nationalism. It is a food that refuses to be tamed, a' eat it may be seen as a "revolutionary" act where one is announcing to whoever bears witness that one is eating a food that has been described as "fearsome" by Western accounts. The power of this imagery is what continues to draw the gaze of millions in social media representations of balut consumption.

The lure to watch balut being consumed in these vlogs, travel shows, and videos may also be aided by a ritualistic aspect to the act of eating it. Viewers of the *Business Insider* video can note the tapping of the egg three times by Ponseca. The ritual patterning of three has been illustrated as the prevalent numerical pattern in American culture (Dundes 1968). After peeling a bit of shell, the typical manner of consumption continues with the sprinkling of salt, which is used in purifying ceremonies, and in the case of balut, also happens to serve as a flavoring agent. Then there is the series of steps or culturally correct way to eat balut which is to first sip the soup, followed by the peeling of the egg and the quick ingestion of the chick and the yolk, with the albumen as the last item to be eaten or discarded due to its texture. This protocol prevents the messiness that ensues when the embryonic duck is taken apart slowly, which is what happens when it is done for maximizing effect as in social media consumption and not for eating for nutrition or enjoyment.

Balut is definitely a food that one has to be culturally introduced to eating (Fernandez, personal communication). Its fluid nature (is it a chick or an egg?) falls outside Western classifications and into the dangerous and "polluting" category as it is not quite whole (Douglas 1966). Therefore to eat it is an unequivocal act that defiantly challenges outsiders and affirms one's status as an insider to Filipino culture (Fernandez 1996a, b; Matejowsky 2013). As a food that illustrates Victor Turner's concept "betwixt and between" (1967), to consume balut is to be incorporated into a group via its successful consumption as a rite-of-passage (Van Gennep [1909] 1965; Matejowsky 2013). This is true for both Filipinos who wish to reaffirm their Filipino identity and for non-Filipinos who desire to be accepted into the local culture or to achieve social and cultural capital. As a liminoid phenomenon, there is more of an option to consume it and less of an obligation. The difference between liminoid and liminal is that "one is all play and choice, an entertainment, the other is a matter of deep seriousness, even dread, it is demanding, compulsory" (Turner 1974:74).

For Filipinos in the diaspora, to eat balut is a chance to choose to affirm citizenship, to indigenize foreign influence, and bring one "home." It carries such strong symbolism that more than any other dish, eating the food that is seen as an object of revulsion in the West affirms a national identity (Ferguson 2010:105). Therefore, the production of balut need not be rooted in the ideal town of Pateros, Philippines, back in the day when ducks ate the snails and wandered freely, but it could be anywhere since it is the act of consuming balut that makes the eater "become" Filipino, an ideological construct. As such, one can see why balut is being used as the vehicle to proclaim national identity since it fits in nicely with the "authenticity" notion that is valued by nationalist agendas and "conceptions of tradition" that are propagated by global movements of OFWs and the interactions with technology such as social media (see De Soucey 2010).

## Balut and nationalist reactions

Comedian Rex Navarrete, who is Filipino American, has joked in his comedy routine about the reluctance of contestants in *Fear Factor* to eat balut even for $50,000, while others who are of Filipino heritage would be more than happy to eat the balut (Navarette 2011). "I want to see our cuisine on the *Food Network*, I'm tired of seeing it on *Fear Factor*. I'm tired. That shit ain't even funny anymore!" (Navarrete 2011).

Like Navarrete, not everyone wants the spotlight on balut or link it to Filipino culture. Chef Andre Guerrero, who owns "The Oinkster," a casual restaurant in Eagle Rock, California which introduced a Filipino purple yam "*ube*" milkshake in the 1990s along with its main menu of American dishes such as pastrami and burger sandwiches, believes Filipino food has to overcome its image as the bizarre cuisine. He blames it on the food media which focuses on the "weird shit" like balut (Spiers 2017):

> With Filipino food, for a long time—and this still happens now—when there's an opportunity to showcase it or talk about it, what do these journalists do? They try to sensationalize the weird shit, like the partially incubated duck egg. OK, you know what? Most of the Filipinos I know don't even eat that. But the way [the media] talk about it, the audience goes, 'Yuck. They eat partially incubated duck eggs and blood soup?' Now they sensationalize it and they've got the audience's attention, but in a very negative way. Why

aren't you talking about the really delicious food that non-Filipinos would embrace and really love? Well, because it's not as interesting.

Romy Dorotan, owner of now-shuttered Cendrillon in New York (one of the first upscale dining restaurants specializing in Filipino cuisine) and the long-standing favorite Purple Yam in Brooklyn, also feels that balut has been misused to the point that for many, it has become identified as being a main part of Filipino cuisine. Although he "loves" balut, he does not intend to put it on the menu at his restaurant. This is because balut "trivializes" the cuisine of the Philippines, he states.

"We will always be known as the cuisine of the weird," Dorotan said in an interview with *The FilAm*, a magazine for Filipino New Yorkers. "I would like Filipino food to be known as healthy, delicious and has variety, but instead what to do we see in some restaurants? The 'balut,' the suckling pig" (Pastor 2015a, b).

Both Rorotan's and Guerrero's comments articulate a different viewpoint from that of Maharlika's owner, Ponseca, who announced her mission to put Filipino food on the map to NBC News on 2014 (National Broadcasting News 2014). Where they differ offers an interesting perspective on what foods are marketed and how they are promoted. Ponseca is of the younger generation adept at using striking visual images which are reality television's hook to lure the curious and she uses foods like balut to overtly proclaim a strong sense of Filipinoness while the other two chef/owners rely on more subtle cues of attractive dishes to interpret what they think Filipino foodways should be. Also pertinent to this discussion is the fact that Maharlika was created in the post-*Fear Factor* period, whereas both Rorotan's and Guerrero's restaurants were established before the advent of social media and omnipresence of reality television.

Ponseca's savvy use of balut to market her restaurant utilizes the food as a tool in a performance that verges on the theatrical (Kirshenblatt-Gimblett 1999). As seen in the video of *Business Insider* where she uses a fork to pick up the fetal duck head, distending its neck toward the camera, Ponseca verges into the region of spectacular entertainment, where the eating is disassociated from nourishment. Eating as a diversion or for amusement is one of the features of experience economy. It is also a demonstration of culinary tourism intentional, exploratory participation in the foodways of an other"

(Long 2004:21). In addition, eating balut becomes not just feeding the body but feeding the performance of the self for those consciously eating it on their path to become self-realized, whether as a plucky foodie, or as a good Filipina citizen who proves her Filipinaness.

Other dishes such as *adobo* may be pleasing to both eye and palate, but despite its status as an unofficial national dish of the Philippines, *adobo* does not have the cultural cachet that balut has, which producers of food/travel shows and YouTube videos, as well as Ponseca, understand. From its humble origin in the Philippines as a cheap street food as common as hot dogs in the United States (Maness 1950), balut has been transformed in the diaspora into something extraordinary that can empower the eater to be somebody who is "doing" or ingesting what celebrities like Anthony Bourdain, Andrew Zimmern, and Gordon Ramsay have experienced.

Reality television and travel shows aided in this transformation, providing viewers the imagination to dream about the possibilities of life and offering maps toward good citizenship (Appadurai 1996; Naccarato and Lebesco 2012). For the fortunate who have the economic and social mobility, indulging in omnivorousness and the pursuit of different foreign cuisines brings culinary capital and accolades from friends and acquaintances (Warde et al. 1999:120). In creating a sense of self in this age of consumption, "what becomes a mark of distinction is not the exclusiveness of one's tastes or choices but rather, an individual's openness to a range of experiences" (Naccarato and Lebesco 2012:9).

The consumption of embryonic eggs also brings up the issue of animal rights, as demonstrated by the petition to ban it. But whether the petition lent illumination to that topic or "shed" light on Filipino culture, what resulted was the free exposure that made more people aware of balut and some of them now want to try it. I suggest that the petition to ban the food imbued even more of a mystique around the fertilized egg; it was now a cause celebré to eat the egg and declare your support for Filipino culture or even better, assert one's right to be a "Filipino" no matter the place.

That balut has become a symbol of the new Filipino movement—and new visibility for the second largest Asian American group in the United States, was confirmed by PJ Quesada, emcee of Pistahan's 2017 balut-eating contest. Shortly before the contest started, he challenged the mixed audience of non-Filipinos and Filipinos alike to take a more active role in promoting the culture. With a microphone in hand, PJ described how balut was used as a "tool of oppression:"

> It says the wrong message. We don't take American food like chitterlings and then put it on *Fear Factor*. It's not fair. What they did is use that food as an example of what Filipinos are like. I just want to point out my objection to that idea. Because Filipinos are awesome. And we eat balut because it's damn good, right? So I encourage everybody, if someone is squeamish about balut. Turn it around. Tell them no, you just don't have a developed palate. And then take them under your wing. Teach them how to eat it. Show them there's nothing to fear about Filipino culture. Can you guys do it for me? Can you do it for Filipino culture? Can you do it for your kids?

PJ's remarks were greeted with cheers and clapping. When interviewed later, PJ recalls saying this. "I remember I was very impassioned when I was saying that." He credits the notion of balut being used as a "tool of oppression" to the late historian Dawn Mabalon who had discussed in a conference he attended how Filipinos were brought in to be displayed in previous World Fairs. The display of Filipinos and other indigenous peoples to bolster the Western attitude regarding the Other has also been considered by other scholars (see Grindstaff 1999; Ku 2013), but Mabalon is widely credited by many in the Filipino American community and others outside it for her activism in bringing to light little-known historical facts involving early Filipino experiences in the United States.

By featuring balut, PJ notes that the reality show provided the general public with its first, contemporary introduction to Filipino cuisine. "It was a grand introduction, but a total disadvantage to the perception of Filipino culture," PJ states. "Whether it was intentional on the producer's part or not ... they wanted to pick out a food that was repulsive to them and showcase that."

By calling on more people to eat balut and teaching others to consume it, PJ's words may be interpreted as marketing the fertilized egg (and Filipino culture) to the audience. He is teaching others to consume it and also relying on culinary tourism to further recruit new eaters. PJ's monologue can also be seen as part of the reclamation of Filipino food from the exoticization that it has been long embellished.

Both PJ's words and Ponseca's statements indicate that negative attention to the delicacy was an assault on Filipino heritage and culture, not just an attack on the food itself (DeSoucey 2010:433). These remarks which indicate gastronationalism at work may have led to the resulting popularity of balut and its consumption. By continuing to serve balut on her menu and making herself accessible to interviews and highlighting the connection between balut and her culture, Ponseca may be seen as capitalizing (or exploiting) on the strong nationalist sentiments swirling around the fertilized egg to bring in people to her restaurant.

Ponseca's marketing strategy using balut also comes at a time when culinary tourism, or the exploration of other people's foodways (Long 2004), is more popular than ever. While eating balut in 2013 as a guest on CNN's *Piers Morgan show*, Anthony Bourdain remarked that "there is a very hot, hipster restaurant currently in New York where hipsters with ironic facial hair and sunglasses are lined up 12 feet to get in and eat this." His statement, a mere observation, nevertheless acted as an affirmation for others that Filipino cuisine is a "cool" thing to try.

The consumption of balut in restaurants or other venues may indeed demonstrate a genuine desire to experience another's culture, but it can also be tied to the issue of cultural food colonialism, when one seeks the most foreign restaurant, to consume foods from non-Western countries without knowing the historical context or caring to know (Heldke 2003). In this case, when non-Filipinos eat the egg to be savvy adventurers or to garner the culinary capital via social media from friends and strangers alike, it can be argued that it is a case of "appropriating" Filipino culture. For those consumers who are of Filipino heritage who post videos of themselves displaying their moment of balut consumption, it can be seen as exploitation of their own culture to gain economic capital, which I will further illustrate in Chapter 5.

PJ's declaration of "chitterlings" (a.k.a. chitlins) as "American food" highlights what some Filipino Americans may think of American food. Made from the intestines of a pig, chitterlings are boiled, stewed, or fried and are eaten in various areas of the world. It is part of the "soul food" culinary tradition of African Americans in the southern United States. As an "ethnic" food, it bears some similarities with balut in that both foods are at once embraced and disavowed by many who belong to these communities. For African Americans, chitterlings, "are both a symbol of racial pride and a source of embarrassment" (Bronner 1981:117), sentiments shared by many Filipino Americans about balut. In any case, chitterlings which require a labor-intensive preparation are not widely available throughout United States and it is not considered a mainstream American food.

PJ's statement about chitterlings implies another issue, one that has to do with the continuing struggle of Filipino Americans to be accepted as "Americans." Chitterlings are usually not featured in reality shows as part of the food challenge for contestants who must prove their mettle, unlike balut. But this may have more to do with the longer history of African Americans in the country and many in the United States are relatively more familiar with soul food than Filipino food. For Filipino Americans, their relative invisibility and integration process into American society which is still in the initiatory stage are factors that make up their "Other-ness" so much so that their foodways is featured in reality television shows as a formidable food to eat.

## The tarnishing of Filipino foodways

PJ's remarks and the reaction of the Filipino community toward the petition to ban balut in the above example did not originate solely from mainstream and social media's portrayal of balut. Filipino American scholars have examined how Filipino food was treated in colonial times and how the foodways of early Filipino migrant workers in the 1920s and 1930s were seen as "barbaric," as demonstrated earlier. This may be interpreted as a form of cultural imperialism where the colonized Filipino people's cultural practices and foodways were subjugated in favor of Western practices and beliefs (Heldke 2003:xvii).

This cultural imperialism which resulted during the colonization of the Philippines by the United States was accompanied by the marginalization of Filipinos in American society. Filipinos in the diaspora and especially Filipino Americans must deal with "the ghosts of colonialism" which lead them to experience and deal with a pervasive sense of dislocation and alienation (Rafael 2002:370).

Filipinos are in a double bind in the United States. "On the one hand, they are racialized in the United States as nonwhite … On the other hand, they are ed to the political and symbolic economies of the United States such eir 'Filipino-ness' remains of dubious authenticity to Filipinos in the

Philippines" (Rafael 2002:371). Filipino Americans' racialization originates from the history of US imperialism and leads many to desire to be "visible" as part of the American story, even as a "sensation" (see Isaac 2006:xviii).

This wanting to be a part of the American narrative has led to the Filipino American media's striking coverage of Gianni Versace's killer Andrew Cunanan, whose Filipino-ness was eagerly called out by the press (Isaac 2006). It may be this very same desire to be a sensation just to be visible that informed my initial delight to see the portrayal of balut on national television. Seeing something of Filipino culture on television was kind of a validation for me. I did not like, however, the fact that the "validating" moment was a biased and partial representation.

Food has long been used by folk groups to construct and denote identity (see Jones 2005). It is usually the community who selects the various types of food to reveal different aspects of that group's identity to the public. Certain foods are chosen to announce a public identity while other foods are kept within the community as these may be seen as disgusting outside the culture (Magliocco 1993). It is generally the case that the merchant selling the food is from that culture and as the cultural broker, she or he gets to decide what food will get represented and what ethnic identity will be communicated (Magliocco 1993; also see Georges 1984).

However, in the case of balut, the reality show producers did not care about whether or not the Filipino American community had a say over how they wish to represent their food to the public. Titillation and high shock value seem to be the deciding factors for what to feature for this show and similar reality television productions. There is no interest in subtle contexts that provide a more accurate depiction of a cultural practice or a nuanced tradition, as there is no room for such in reality television, and increasingly, in American popular culture and society where outrageousness is harnessed for economic and cultural capital by people of all types. In this climate, balut, arguably found the most "offensive" food by most Americans, was the one that was showcased. Thus, the grand introduction of Filipino food in the beginning of twenty-first century to the Western audience was this street food which, intentionally or not, became the stereotypical first impression that many had about Filipino cuisine.

The complex feelings of *hiya* and embarrassment Filipinos feel over f such as balut is worsened for many each time balut is portrayed in a ne light in some television show or YouTube video. Such depictions deliberately tie the fertilized egg to the Philippines, and by extension, to the Filipino diasporic population despite its prevalence in other Southeast nations. Balut, a food considered by Filipinos as an "insider" food, became by force, a food for "overt display" (Magliocco 1993). It became a signifier of Filipino identity (Barthes 1997), and Other-ness for those outside the culture.

Filipino American presence is only beginning to be noticed as the second largest Asian American group in the United States. Their cultural practices and their foodways are still painted with the foreign patina that hangs around ethnic groups still lobbying for acceptance in mainstream America. It was only around 2017 when respected restaurant critic Jonathan Gold announced that Filipino cuisine was having a moment in fine dining (Gold 2017). Before then, Filipino cuisine in the United States was mostly relegated to fast-casual eateries were dishes were inexpensive and the stylistic touches to dishes were limited. These were called *"turo-turo"* (point-point) joints were one pointed to the dishes in steamed trays and the emphasis was not on the way it looked but how it tasted and was it close enough to what Filipino Americans cooked at home.

Chain restaurants that opened up in the United States made up another kind of Filipino restaurant that were (and still are) found in both sides of the coast and in some big cities. The list includes Goldilocks Bakeshop which opened in 1976 in Los Angeles, Max's Restaurant which is now run by the third generation of owners serving up its famous fried chicken and other Filipino dishes, Barrio Fiesta which emphasized traditional cuisine in a formal setting, and Jollibee restaurant which has 34 locations across the United States offering its menu of "Filipinized" hamburgers, sweet-tasting spaghetti, and fried offerings.

Now that the Filipino cuisine is on the radar of foodies, there is a new type of Filipino restaurant available in the United States: the upscale, fine dining establishments that are marked by fusion and creative touches from chefs of Filipino heritage who have been trained in French techniques and who have only recently become encouraged to cook their own cuisine. This list includes Lasa and Ma'am Sir in Los Angeles and Bad Saint in Washington DC which was named as no. 2 best new restaurant in 2016 by *Bon Appetit* magazine. It seems to those observing the restaurant scene that Filipino food seems to have hit the mainstream (Mishan 2018).

Despite these promising signs, Filipino food still has a long way to go in its journey away from the "ethnic" factor. Part of the reason why it is considered as the "in" cuisine at the moment is due to the fact that it has long been misunderstood and ignored, and its exotic factor appeals to the omnivore's desires to consume it in an act that may be construed as cultural food colonialism (Heldke 2003). Perhaps when there are an abundance of Filipino restaurants in every state like there are Japanese or Chinese restaurants, or even Thai eateries, will the cuisine be truly "mainstream."

## Culinary nationalism and the Filipino food moment

More than a decade after the 2002 debut of balut, it appears that its treatment, at least in conventional media, may be changing. Signs that it is transforming is evident in the way that Filipino restaurants are being publicized in the current foodie discourse. The tone of coverage may well have been changed by the media influence of celebrity chefs like Andrew Zimmern. Zimmern went on the record on 2012 during his television show *Bizarre Foods* that Filipino food was "the next best thing." Although Zimmern may have been off by a few years, PJ agrees with his prediction, noting that Filipino food has been represented in the media more fairly since 2012. Zimmern's prediction helped map the next destination for food adventurers to follow on their quest for culinary tourism.

Besides the influence wielded by celebrities like Andrew Zimmern which has translated into broader coverage and desire for Filipino food, leading to the opening of a number of upscale Filipino restaurants which have not existed before this Filipino food moment, another factor changing the way that such foods as balut is discussed may be due to how marginalized Filipino Americans are talking back about their foods and culture. The culinary nationalism that is currently fomenting, along with the present Filipino food moment, is an attempt to take back control over what may be seen as cultural appropriation of Filipino food.

The representation or possessing of another person's cultural heritage without proper context has been remarked elsewhere (Heldke 2003; Ray 2016). But what happens when the individual who is doing the "borrowing" is from that culture? In that case, it can be seen as more of a marketing of culinary nationalism that results in profiting from the foodie's search for authenticity.

It can also be understood as an attempt to locate the authentic in one's culture, whether in its practices or in its cuisine. If true, this illustrates how "the search for authenticity is fundamentally an emotional and moral quest" (Bendix 1997:7).

In "Eating the Other: Desire and Resistance," belle hooks writes of the continuing fascination with racial difference, where the "commodification of Otherness" continues to be profitable as it is promoted "as a new delight, more intense, more satisfying than normal ways of doing and feeling" (366). Whether it is a Filipino restaurateur who is gaining clientele and media exposure from the use of balut to trumpet cultural difference or reality television producers portraying balut in a savage light, it may be seen as attempts to commodify "otherness" in pursuit of economic gain.

For those groups who have been subjected to marginalization, and largely been invisible in mainstream society such as Filipinos, hooks charges that they "can be seduced by the emphasis on Otherness, by its commodification, because it offers the promise of recognition and reconciliation" (370). Despite what may seem to be actual political change and the achievement of the American Dream where those who were once outside are finally included, what may be occurring instead is "essentialist cultural nationalism" that if questioned, is but a familiar form drawing on stereotypes of the Other and not actual engaged interrogation of what led to those very stereotypes (hooks 370).

However this may be, I am not quick to dismiss the culinary nationalism being exhibited by restaurateurs or in other venues like festivals as occurrences that do not qualify as real resistance. I like to think it can be a kind of resistance than can beget change for a few, fortunate groups via economic and culinary capital. If Otherness is used as a lure to bring in people to eat foods they otherwise may not try, then that can be used to bring in transformative moments where the diner may be subjected to learning not just what the food she or he is eating from, but where it came from and what migratory movements, colonial upheavals, and political forces caused it to bring the food to the plate. This is much like what happened in the California food movement that was first forged in the dining rooms such as Alice Water's Chez Panisse in Berkeley in the early 1970s.

Through the commodification of cultural practices such as balut-eating, money flows in along with cultural capital. The recipients of this flow, restaurateurs of Filipino-themed restaurants, chefs of Filipino heritage, any savvy foodie from other ethnicities, gain economic and culinary capital that they can parlay into more recognition for their platform.

If indeed, the Filipino food movement is true to its goals to bring attention to Filipinos in America and to promote the culture and cuisine, then that platform created can offer real change for select, privileged members in this community of immigrants. They need not feel "*hiya*" or shame any longer.

3

# The Sensual and Supernatural in Balut Lore

*"The manananggal [aswang] (a succubus creature) came about eating balut"*
—K.K, realtor, Filipino

*"Like Viagra for men"*
—A, 46, artist, second-generation Filipino

These two statements from my online survey in 2017 on balut hint at a rich folklore associated with the fertilized egg and its ingestion. This chapter will be devoted to exploring the rich symbolism and beliefs associated with the foodways of balut, which ranges from the supernatural to the sensual. By providing the background of balut's role in folk beliefs, the significant position that this food occupies in the culture is made more tangible and further illustrates why it has been used as a marker for Filipino-ness.

The notion of balut as the food of the Other is further expanded below, with the Other referring to the marginalized as well as to those considered beyond human. I refer to the belief that a few of the balut survey respondents noted about the embryonic egg being a food of the *aswang*, a legendary, self-segmenting creature that feeds on people's entrails. Known as a supernatural being who consumes the viscera or organs of human beings, the belief in the existence of the *aswang* is found throughout Southeast Asia. In the Philippines, however, the *aswang* is usually portrayed as a woman (Figure 15). The gendering of this supernatural creature occurred during Spanish colonization of the archipelago, when missionaries effectively cast the once-powerful indigenous female shamans known as the *baylan* as the *aswang* in an effort to take away their respected status (Menez 1996). In addition, the connection between the supernatural to sexual beliefs via balut is also addressed below

**Figure 15** Drawing rendition of an *aswang* creature with balut—Courtesy of Leah Kohler.

by exploring the fertilized egg's reputation as an aphrodisiac solely for men. Through the consumption of balut, some men perform a machismo-tinged masculinity that effectively excludes women from being agents of their own sexuality.

Balut encapsulates how food can be both democratic and a way to be distinct in today's world (Johnston and Baumann 2010:xv). It is also used as a way to mark boundaries separating insiders and outsiders. Like the crayfish that has become the ethnic and regional symbol for Cajuns in South Louisiana and a way to distinguish them from non-Cajuns (Gutierrez 1984), so has balut become a way to prove one is a "Filipino" and stand out from the rest.

Demonstrating food's ability to communicate multivalent meanings, balut is also a food that can mark those who are outside mainstream Philippine society—the "*aswang*" of the culture—such as widows or strangers who have been relegated to the fringes of their communities. In addition, balut has become a food that can signal other behaviors (see Barthes 1997), when eating it signifies an increase in sexual energy for men. Although it is eaten by children and adults in the Philippines, by those who are ailing or in need of an energy boost, in the United States, it is also eaten by men of Filipino heritage (and increasingly non-Filipino background) in drinking events as a natural "Viagra." This aphrodisiac enables them to achieve cultural and social capital among peers. Whether used as an aphrodisiac or manipulated into a tool of "othering," interpreting balut's multivocal meanings exemplify how food can transform itself to indicate a situation.

"*Food has a constant tendency to transform itself into situation*" (Barthes 1997:26, his emphasis). In the case of balut, it is no longer just an embryonic food snack but rather a food that can signify a circumstance, whether a social drinking event or a sexually boosting energizer. It can stand in for relaxation time as well as being a signifier of Otherness. In the Philippines, the "Other" can refer to the marginalized members of the society.

Although balut can be eaten by men, women, and children, men are consistently believed to be the ones who can benefit from the aphrodisiac quality allegedly in balut, based on fieldwork results. The belief in the sexual function of balut was evident from both genders, but responses indicated that it is for men only—a case of gendering when it comes to the sexual benefits of balut. Yet for other alleged benefits of balut, such as its nutritious value, both genders related that the egg is nutritious for men and women.

For most of my study participants, confronting the sight of the developed chick in the shell was uncomfortable. With the average person more familiar with processed meat in gleaming Styrofoam packages, eating something that clearly resembles the animal can be a challenge for some who do not want to be reminded of what they are eating. The uneasiness that occurs when balut is encountered is not limited to individuals outside the culture. Even some within the culture find balut to be unsavory, which may explain why the most common way to eat balut is two to three bites, and not linger over the sight.[1]

An embryonic duck with folded wings and developed eyes nestled in the moist folds of its yolk is not an easy sight to behold. Whether 17 days or 21 days, the fertilized egg has progressed to the point that it is clearly a bird about to be hatched. Even when not developed into balut, eggs can sometimes provoke apprehension in some individuals due to the fact that they represent life.

Venetia Newall in her tour-de-force work on eggs, modestly titled *An Egg at Easter*, observed "the universal significance of an egg as an image of the life force" (1971:113). As one example of the egg as representative of life, the Emu peoples from central Australia abstained from eggs from their tribal totem even during food shortages, as they believed "the life of the totem" lives in the egg (Newall 1971:114). Young women residing in northern Nigeria were forbidden to eat eggs, as to eat them would destroy "a symbol of life" and to do so would make them barren (Newall 1971:114–115).

Fertilized eggs with developed embryos in them may be seen as even more of "an image of the life force" (Newall 1971:113), even for those who eat balut as part of their cultural practice. To eat balut, then, is to risk being judged harshly by those who believe it is wrong to eat a creature that was never given the chance to live. This gives rise to events such as the petition to ban balut, as detailed in the previous chapter. In addition, although balut-eating is a traditional practice, it has also been used by some as a form of judgment against others in the Philippines.

Some narratives about balut associate the consumption of it to an ostracized group within Filipino society, the elderly widow or stranger to the community who have been deemed an *"aswang"* (also spelled *asuang*) by those around them. The *aswang* is a supernatural creature that is known by other names in places such as Indonesia, Melanesia, and the Trobiand Islands. In the Philippines, an *aswang* is usually portrayed as a woman whose favorite foods include the unborn. The belief in the *aswang* can sometimes lead to fatal results. Numerous Philippine newspaper accounts describe the beatings or murders of unfortunate people believed to be an *aswang*.

On November 2, 2005, a widow suspected of being a "witch" was hacked death while preparing her supper in Pangasinan, Philippines (Visperas 5);

- On July 4, 2009, a 70-year-old, half-blind elderly woman accused of being an *aswang* was found molested and stabbed to death in her makeshift home in Negros Occidental (Bayoran 2009);
- On July 24, 2014, a man beheaded his 70-year-old mother in Bacolod City, Philippines, claiming she was an *aswang* with her changing looks (Gomez 2014);
- On September 4, 2014, a man in Bacolod City killed his 74-year-old neighbor, whom he accused as being an *aswang* due to "eerie experiences" (Lopez 2014).

As these news stories of victims being murdered due to the belief in the *aswang* illustrate, the *aswang* belief continues to flourish in present-day Philippines. This is not surprising as "personal supernatural experience narrative doesn't exist *in the face of* modern scientific knowledge, but in content and structure it exists *because* of modern scientific knowledge" (Goldstein 2007:78). In fact, some aspects of the *aswang* phenomenon are connected to the experience of sleep paralysis (Hufford 1982:236). Beliefs in ghosts and other supernatural entities are widely disseminated by mass media, popular culture as well as technology and continue to be generated in part because of this relationship (Goldstein, Grider and Thomas 2007). Therefore, it should be no surprise that belief in the *aswang* still holds court in Filipino culture. Since this is a balut study, it is necessary to discuss other aspects of what the consumption of it is believed to do for some, which is to turn one into an *aswang*.

## Defining the *aswang*

Because there are thousands of islands in the Philippines and many languages, it is not surprising that there are various names for this creature, depending on the region and the type of *aswang* (see Lieban 1967:68; Ramos 1969: 238; Ramos 1990b:xvi–xvii). I will be dealing mostly with the type known as the viscera-sucker (or one who eats human organs), characterized as the most malevolent one of all (Menez 1996:86). The following are a list of common names for the viscera-sucker *aswang* including *abat* (Waray), *aswang na lupad* (flying aswang, Bikol), *boroka* (Iloko, from Spanish word "bruja"), *manananggal* (Tagalog), *mangalok* (Cuyonon), *naguneg* (Iloko), *laman luob* (Tagalog), and *kasudlan* (West Visayan) (Ramos 1990a:142, 1990b:xviii).

One of the most terrifying aspects of this creature in the tales and legends concerns its appetite for the unborn. In the Philippines, legends featuring the female *aswang* describe its penchant to suck out babies from their mothers' wombs via a long tubular, proboscis-like tongue that penetrates into the expectant mothers' naval or any other orifice in order to suck out the baby. The *aswang* can also use its sharpened nails to slice open the womb of its victim to retrieve the unborn child, said to be the *aswang's* favorite food. Pregnant women are believed to emit the scent of a ready-to-eat jackfruit (Demetrio 1971:239, 245) and because of this, the *aswang* can find soon-to-be mothers easily in the dark night.

Although it can seem to be an ordinary person by day, at night, the *aswang* transforms and sheds its lower body to hide it in a clump of banana trees or anywhere it can camouflage or hide its lower half. With the help of foul oils rubbed in its armpits, the *aswang* changes its arms into wings and its once-luxurious hair becomes thickened propellants, allowing the creature to fly with its entrails trailing beneath it. Once it spots a likely place to land, it perches onto the roof where it unfurls its lengthy and tubular tongue (Menez 1996:86). The tongue penetrates past thatched roofs or through cracks in the window to "suck out the internal organs of a person asleep or an infant inside its mother below" (Ramos 1990a:140).

An *aswang* can also position itself under the bamboo floor of a nipa hut, directly underneath the bed of the sick where it feeds on the phlegm of the person afflicted with tuberculosis or similar illness. Those who are good-looking strangers, or widows, or an elderly person can be suspected of being an *aswang*, as well as visitors from other villages or regions. Indeed, the *aswang* fear has been blamed for the "divisive tendencies among Philippine groups" (Ramos 1990b:xviii).

But one is not powerless against the *aswang*. There are tools, weapons if you will, that can destroy it. These include salt, spices, or vinegar that if sprinkled on the lower half of the viscera-sucker can render it powerless and kill it while it is still segmented. A sting ray's tail, knives, and the bamboo stick can also be used to destroy it (Ramos 1990b:xxi–xx).

In Melanesia, this creature is believed to use pandanus leaves to fly, or its own hair and ears (Ramos 1990a:144). In Indonesia, it is called *"tanggal"* (the word *"tanggal"* means to detach, or unfasten in Tagalog, Indonesian, and Malaysian). However, in these places as well as in the areas of the Philippines such as southern Mindanao and in the mountains of Northern Luzon where Spanish colonization was less successful, the viscera-sucker *aswang* is normally depicted as a bird or a dog-like creature, not a woman (Menez 1996:87). Instead, the feminization of the viscera-sucker is commonly found among Filipino societies such as the lowland Christians, and it is generally absent in areas where the animist beliefs remain strong (Menez 1996:87).

One of the most popular sources on the *aswang* which cements Goldstein and colleagues' point that mass media and technology bolster and sustain supernatural beliefs (2007) is the documentary called *The Aswang Phenomenon* (2011), made by Canadian filmmaker Jordan Clark. Clark sets out to investigate what is an *aswang* in the Philippines, and its tenacious hold on many Filipinos. He interviews a variety of writers, artists, and other individuals about their ideas regarding the creature. The majority of those interviewed agreed that although an *aswang* may take shape in many forms, it was unanimously associated with evil. Among those featured in the film was director Peque Gallaga, who notes, "I like the *aswang* idea because it is so amorphous, ambiguous, and it is unknown."

These characteristics of ambiguity and amorphousness are shared by balut, as it is neither an egg nor a duck, but a creature of liminality poised at the stage of in-between where it is still evolving and changing. Such things (including beings in transition, such as the *aswang*) are perceived as dangerous (Douglas 1966). This quality of "danger" amplifies the daring-ness of ingesting balut. Which is why to eat it on Western television is more likely to be received as a "stunt," especially when the consumption of it is framed as such the very first time it was presented to millions of Americans.

Describing how balut was featured in the show *Fear Factor*, literature scholar Vivian Halloran states that contestants must "overcome their olfactory, gustatory, and cultural repulsion and eat an item existentially suspended between the categories of the cooked and the raw, to paraphrase Lévi-Strauss, as well as between life (symbolized by the egg) and death (made manifest by the presence of bones)" ([1966] Halloran 2004:37). As a creature of liminality, balut is a food that is cloaked in mystery and intrigue, much like the *aswang*. With these shared characteristics, it is fitting that balut plays a critical role in transforming a person into an *aswang*, according to Philippine lore.

The *aswang* was already a belief in existence when the Spanish landed in the sixteenth century. In 1582, Spanish explorer Miguel de Loarca wrote about the *aswang* belief prevalent among the Pintados of Panay. In 1588–1591, Juan de Plasencia described the Tagalogs of Luzon and how they believed in the *aswang*. These accounts indicate that the Spanish did not bring the concept of the *aswang* to the Philippines.

With Magellan's arrival, however, the *aswang* became associated with respected female *baylan* (shamans, healers) as an attempt by the colonizers to control the women's high status and sexuality (Menez 1996). According to folklorist Herminia Menez, the Spaniards "dealt with recalcitrant female shamans not only as their religious rivals but as females whose sexual powers, in their view, needed to be subjugated under male authority" (1996:88).

## Creating the *aswang* legend

Drawing primarily from the Spanish chronicles written by missionaries from the Jesuit, Augustinian, and Franciscan orders, Menez reveals how the *baylan* were demonized due to their attempts to defend their indigenous animist beliefs. The *baylan* were influential and formidable religious leaders and prophetesses, seen on par with the headhunting male chiefs. For example, the *baylan* of the Kalinga-Buaya tribe of Northern Luzon officiated religious ceremonies and decided the time and location of headhunting attacks, even throwing the first spear (Menez 1996:88).

However, the *baylan* in the Spanish chronicles were painted as lascivious, immoral women who were in league with the devil in their pagan beliefs (Menez 1996:91). In reaction to the women's defense of their animist faith, the Spanish colonizers conducted mass conversions. When their attempts were unsuccessful, "they burned their idols and sacred groves" (Menez 1996:91). Thanks to their tenacious attempts to wipe out indigenous beliefs by persecuting the *baylan*, the Spanish colonial officials somewhat succeeded in depicting once-respected chiefesses and prophetesses as liminal creatures of the underworld.

As of the 1990s, however, there were still areas in the Philippines where the *aswang* belief had not gained a stronghold. Remarking on the presence of garlic (one of the tools to destroy an *aswang*), in the houses as well as businesses all throughout Ilocos Norte, Gilda Cordero-Fernando writes that garlic is intended for buyers, not as *aswang* deterrents (1992). Indeed, Ilocos Norte is a renowned garlic-producing area in the Philippines. Cordero-Fernando states that "Ilocanos are used to strong women. They need them, are not afraid of them and therefore, do not convert them into *aswang*" (1992:144). With the rise of technology and films like *The Aswang Phenomenon*, one can surmise that more areas of the country, and the world, will become exposed to the notion of the *aswang* as a woman. The exposure of the belief, disseminated widely by mass media and technology, would then generate and sustain more *aswang* lore (Goldstein, Grider and Thomas 2007).

In addition to the concerted efforts to erase the animist belief systems they encountered, Spanish missionaries also deliberately took the characteristics attributed to the native prophetesses and healers and instead, inverted those same traits so that the once-powerful women were now associated with the vile *aswang*. Using Filipino narratives, Menez illustrates how the motifs in the stories emphasize "inversions" that can be related to how female shamans in pre-colonial Philippines were subverted by the Spanish (1996:88).

Inversions can be seen in the following examples. The *baylan* were originally known to use sweet-scented oils as integral to their presence and tools of their healing repertoire. In contrast, the *aswang* is a corruption of this tradition, emitting a foul odor that announces its manifestation. As a healer and midwife, the *baylan* who was trusted for her curative and restorative powers transformed as the *aswang* who thrives on the phlegm of the sick and instead of delivering babies, "drains the fetus out of the womb" (Menez 1996:89). In the *aswang*, the "opposition between life taking and life giving, between killing and birthing, is underscored by the self-segmenting process in which the reproductive half is left behind while the upper half is engaged in death-dealing activity" (Menez 1996:89). With such inversions and the zealous destruction of any remnants of animist beliefs, the Spanish attempted to diminish the power and status of the native women.

## Balut and the *aswang*

Through the centuries, the *aswang* belief has evolved to now refer to something or someone that is evil. Although there are multiple routes to become an *aswang*, some of the most prominent involve balut. One way is for the desiring person to place a "fertilized chicken egg against his/her belly and then tie it in place with a cloth around the body. After an unspecified time, the chicken from the egg passes into the stomach by a sort of osmosis. Then one becomes able to emit the sound characteristic of the *aswang*" (Ramos 1971:121).

Another striking method takes place at night in a cemetery during Good Friday, the day Jesus is believed to have died according to the Christian tradition. The inductee takes two fertilized eggs and then must "stand erect, gaze directly at the full moon without closing one's eyes, place an egg under one's armpit, and mumble certain words ... when the egg disappeared into the initiate's stomach, he had become an *aswang*" (Ramos 1971:122).

A third method involves not balut, but a fully formed, black chick which must be swallowed when it is discharged from a dying viscera-sucker (Ramos 1973:21). Once swallowed, the chick lives in the new *aswang*'s stomach and will feed on whatever its host eats. The *aswang*'s hunger for human entrails is activated "when the chick starts cheeping" (Ramos 1990a:144, 1973:21). It is worth repeating here that balut eggs that have turned black are considered to be bad, and that Filipinos prefer the less developed balut to eat.

Out of a total of 46 participants in the two surveys replying to the question whether they knew of any folklore related to balut, five individuals, all women, provided a reply regarding the *aswang* belief.[2] A 38-year-old woman noted that when she ate balut, she felt like someone from the provincial areas known to harbor the *aswang*. Another respondent, a 58-year-old, stated that although there is no connection between balut and the *aswang*, the *aswang* reside in the Visayan province of Capiz. For 60-year-old K.K., an *aswang* is created from eating balut, while 40-year-old P.P. compared eating balut to being "almost like cannibalism."

P.P. was born in the United States but once resided in Antique, one of four provinces in the island of Panay. Besides Antique, the other provinces are Iloilo, Aklan, and Capiz, all places reputed to be *aswang* territory (see Ramos 1971:108, 1990b:136). P.P. noted that she believed that the Spaniards named the place as such because they could perceive the "antique" nature of the place. Belief in the supernatural is common, with the *wak-wak* known as a type of bird aswang (see De Jesus ed. 1986:14, 24–25, 30; Gonzalez-Tabujara 1985:97, 103–104).

For three years, P.P. lived in Antique with her family and ate balut regularly at least twice a month. When she was expecting her first child, she consumed balut daily. She noted that balut is a food that provides energy to those who need it, including the *aswang*. Describing a balut egg, P.P. noted the following:

> When you look at balut, you see the veins, the skin, the fetus inside. It's like you're eating a human fetus. I can see where eating balut can empower an *aswang*, since *aswangs* like to eat the fetuses of human babies.

The idea that balut consumption can invest an *aswang* with power can be analyzed using the principles of sympathetic magic, as outlined by James Frazer in his work, *The Golden Bough* (1935, third edition). Although Frazer's evolutionary theoretical stance has since been discredited, his theory on the sympathetic principle continues to be relevant, and examples of it abound in films and in literature such as J.K. Rowling's Harry Potter series where the evil Voldemort's soul is stored in a Horcrux, an object that safeguards it. Destroying that Horcrux is to destroy Voldemort, which demonstrates Frazer's idea that "like produces like," or homeopathic magic.

Many aphrodisiacs are associated with the principle of homeopathy (Jones 2005) but balut also involves the principle of contagious magic, or "law of contact," which is another tenet of sympathetic magic. Frazer defines this as the idea that a relation or "sympathy" will be still present between objects which were once connected despite separation. Clothing belonging to an individual or that person's strand of hair or fingernail cuttings are thought to continue to hold power over that person as these were once connected to that individual. A wax figure which resembles a person and contains his/her hair or piece of clothing combines principles of homeopathic and contagious magic; therefore, the doll is believed to be extra potent.

In consuming balut, these two tenets of magic are also involved. This is illustrated by the belief that if one eats balut, which is a developing chick, then the result will be more energy due to the incorporation of the chick's animating force. Balut is prescribed and recommended to those who are ailing or in need of extra boost such as students preparing for final exams.

It is also recommended especially to men who would like to have a more energetic sex life. If the principles of magic are applied in this case, for men who eat balut as "*pangpalakas ng tuhod*" (to strengthen the knees), the interpretation may be that for these men, eating balut enables them to receive the life force of the baby chick which they can now use to improve their stamina. As these above examples illustrate, Frazer's explanation of sympathetic magic remains insightful.

For individuals who are marginalized from mainstream Filipino society, such as the elderly widow or a stranger in a village, being associated with balut may prove to be negative. Although balut is sold more and more in stationary stalls, there are still itinerant vendors. In certain parts of the Philippines, such peripatetic vendors, especially those from the Western Visayas, are treated with hostility and may be seen as the *aswang*. They are believed to be *aswang* disguised as vendors selling wares so that they can find prey such as expectant mothers (Ramos 1990b:xxiv–xxv). Such beliefs affect other customs, such as the sharing of food. Although it is customary to generously share food among friends and family, "where the *aswang* belief persists, Filipinos seldom accept gifts of food from strangers" (Ramos 1990b:xxv).

Homeopathic and contagious magic may also be used in one interpretation of why the *aswang*'s favorite food would be a fetus. In eating the unborn, it is believed that the *aswang* can absorb the fetus's life energy. Consuming the vital organs such as the liver, spleen, and heart of its victims, an *aswang* is capable of ensuring its health and continuing existence. If the sympathetic magic interpretation is also applied to the *aswang*'s tendency to nourish on the phlegm and diseased and dying, it can also be seen as a way that the *aswang* is a "dead" creature by feeding on such materials.

Mary Douglas theorized on the concepts of purity and pollution across cultures, and how these notions illuminate the meaning behind food taboos. Pollution in a culture is tied to a "total structure of thought" (Douglas 1966:41). Wholeness of body and unity is considered holy, while something that is anomalous is seen as unclean (Douglas 1966:54). Anomalous things, much like an *aswang* which feeds on bodily emissions and entrails, represents unholiness and disorder. By applying the principles of pollution and taboo as noted by Douglas, the *aswang* grows more dangerous and powerful in its disordered state with each sip of the polluting phlegm as a creature betwixt and between (Douglas 1966; Turner 1967).

The fifth participant, who noted a connection between balut and the *aswang*, was 22-year-old female student I.Y. who provided more extensive answers. I.Y. described her childhood during the 1980s in Quezon City, Philippines, where she was born and how balut was a favorite snack.

She recalled the hurtful teasing she received from other children who would see her eating balut. "*Oh, aswang ka, aswang ka!! Kadiri ka, kadiri ka!!*" (Oh, you're an aswang, aswang!! You're gross, you're gross!!) was an unfortunate taunt she received as a 10-year old. To deflect the teasing, I.Y. would respond by retorting that since she was going to be an *aswang*, she would make sure to capture them. According to I.Y., she learned her reply from other children as this was a common response.

She also shared her belief that children who consumed balut were subjected to more ridicule than adults. "If children are seen eating balut, the reaction is more strong as opposed to adults eating the balut, because the child is vulnerable and is preying on something vulnerable," I.Y. stated. According to I.Y.'s interpretation, the partially developed chick in balut can be seen as defenseless and vulnerable, and this links the idea of eating balut to the *aswang* belief as the *aswang* likes to feast on the susceptible including the helpless babies in their mothers' wombs.

The insult that I.Y. was subjected to is a taunt that continues to be in practice for some Filipino Americans. In 2010, I witnessed this first hand while waiting in line at an Asian grocery store in Los Angeles, California. Ahead of me was a Filipino American woman who stepped out temporarily to retrieve an item from the shelf. When she came back, another woman, also Filipino American, had taken her place. During their angry discussion, the first woman called the line interloper an "*aswang*" as she stole her position in line. The insult struck a nerve and they continued to argue. Clearly, an *aswang* in this context is anyone who has behaved in an antisocial manner. Being antisocial is to be outside the norms of society which thrives on order. Such behavior promotes a disordered state, implying that the interloper is both dangerous and powerful (Douglas 1966).

Another interesting parallel which connects balut-eating to the *aswang* belief is the common practice to eat balut at night. The legends about the *aswang* creature stipulate that it feeds on its vulnerable victims also at night. For most of my study participants, eating balut was something done quickly as they admitted not wanting to see the balut chick they are eating. It is usually swallowed without too much time devoted to looking at the food. Eating balut at night is also common in the Philippines, perhaps because under the cover of darkness, it is hard for the balut-eater to see what he or she is eating. In doing so, the balut-eater is obscuring the fact, whether intentional or not, that he or she is eating an embryonic chick. Another interpretation could be that the darkness also is a cover for the balut-eater to indulge in a favorite snack without being judged by others. The night essentially acts like a protective cover for the balut-eater.

## The social life of balut

The answers of my balut study participants illustrate that the preferred way of eating balut is with others, thereby emphasizing that the social aspect of eating it cancels out whatever negative connotations may linger about balut being the food of the Other, in this case, the *aswang*. All 26 participants who answered the question "who do you eat balut with, yourself or with others?" remarked they ate balut with other people, family and friends. It is a social food, which contrasts with the *aswang* feeding alone at night.

Whether it is served in an egg cup accompanied with beer or a cocktail as in the Maharlika restaurant in New York, or in countless parties at home or as a fun, pick-me-up appetizer after work with family and *barkada* (friends), balut is usually not devoured alone and in private. When it is done alone, eating balut can conjure up primal images that may be disconcerting.

Said one male participant who shared that he ate balut with friends and also alone, "Sometimes I like to eat it by myself in a dark room while I pretend I am a wild animal and I am stealing the young of other avian animals and I viciously consume their young in front of the parents. Lol." Although some eateries have tried to serve balut as a main dish, the traditional and preferred way it is consumed is as a side dish or appetizer in drinking sessions.

Balut may be seen as one of those foods that can be classified as "raw" and needs cultural mediation in order for it to be "cooked" (Levi Strauss [1966] 2008). In *The Culinary Triangle*, Levi Strauss analyzes cultural methods of cooking, with boiling considered a cultural mediation due to the use of the receptacle, a cultural object ([1966] 2008:37). Extending this idea further, the consumption of balut with family and friends further "cooks" the embryonic egg. The social ritual whether in the form of parties or drinking events such as *inuman* requires its own code of behavior which "civilizes" a food that has the power to invoke images of the savage *aswang*.

The cultural importance of drinking events called *inuman* was remarked upon centuries ago in the Spanish chronicles replete with the description of numerous alcoholic drinks made from a variety of local ingredients such as bananas, coconuts, and sugar cane which were drunk in rituals to mark rites-of-passage events such as weddings and deaths (Garcia 1979:262, 331). Drinking was also done to honor visitors as well as deities, and a feast was designated by the term referring to "drinking," instead of a word to mean "eating" (Garcia 1979:262).

According to the seventeenth-century historian and Jesuit priest named Pedro Chirino, who described the indigenous people now known as Filipinos, a normal drinking feast at that time consisted of the following:

> They eat, sitting in a low position … without covering or napkins, the plates containing the victuals being placed on the table itself. They eat in groups of sufficient number to surround the table; and it may happen that a house is filled from one end to another with tables, and guests drinking. The food is placed all together upon various plates, and they have no hesitation in putting the hands of all into the same dish, or in drinking out of the same vessel. They eat but little, drink often, and spend much time in the feast. (as quoted in Garcia 1979:262)

Fast forward several centuries later to an *inuman*, with men and women, and their *barkada*. The setting could be in the home around a table in the kitchen or on the wooden tables and benches outside a local sari-sari store in the Philippines. Alcohol and finger foods or *pulutan* including balut are served and enjoyed together in a convivial atmosphere. Such an event results in one feeling energized with improved blood circulation, feeling "active and revitalized" (Cabotaje 1976:109).

When eating balut within the context of such a gathering, food and performance are woven together. One is behaving in the culturally appropriate way in observing the etiquette of a social event where balut is not the main dish, but only one of the foods served in an atmosphere of congeniality. Although such social occasions as drinking get-togethers are not formal events, there is still a set of precepts that are "performed" by the eater (Kirshenblatt-Gimblett 1999).

Most of the balut study participants described the same feelings of energy and sociability when consuming balut with family and friends. The social aspect of enjoying balut, whether in festivals as will be covered in the next chapter, or in parties and drinking sessions, underscores the sense of community that prevails when it is eaten within context. During such occasions as get-togethers, the setting of the table, procurement of favorite snacks, and the playing of music to fix the mood are all components that make up an *inuman*, an informal ritual. In answer to the question "where do you eat it?" many respondents noted they enjoy it during special occasions. Within this unspoken framework which governs events such as parties or feasts, consumption of balut becomes a culturally sanctioned process, where one is able to consume without fear of being made into an *aswang* Other.

The cultural practice of eating balut in the right context is expected even in the way it is sold. Ambient balut sellers are now rivaled by stationary vendors in the Philippines who are able to form personal relationships with their customers, who can become their *suki* (regulars). The vendor provides the correctly aged balut which is preferred by their *suki*. But for those who buy balut in transportation centers during times of travel where there is no time to foster a relationship with local vendors, balut that is too developed for most is deliberately sold by those "who will never see their customers again, will not hear recriminations, or form friendships with them" (Fernandez 1994:10). The act of selling balut becomes purely one motivated by economic capital. The social as well as cultural factors governing relationship dynamics are left out when the vendor is forcing his or her hapless customer to emulate an *aswang* by selling an already full-formed chick.

To repeat, the more fully formed chick in the balut, the more it is considered culturally unacceptable as most Filipinos prefer a 17-day-old chick or younger. In comparison, an *aswang* harbors "a black, chick-like creature" and the hunger for entrails is initiated once "the chick starts cheeping" (Ramos 1990a:144). 
interpretation of this may be that the more a chick is formed and
:d, the more the host is like an *aswang* with a desire to consume the

flesh of others. If interpreted symbolically, this could be also seen as explaining the cultural belief that balut is an aphrodisiac for men.

## Ethnographic interpretations of eating balut: A natural Viagra?

Called "hard-core balut eaters" by balut distributor Butch Coyoca, male consumers of balut are generally not bothered by the sight of bigger embryos. On the other hand, women prefer to eat balut that is less developed, perhaps strengthening the cultural belief that balut benefits male virility. A balut that is more developed has essentially more meat, and this cultural preference upholds a Westernized form of masculinity where men are expected to eat more meat and women tend to minimize or abstain from it (Calvert 2014; Sumpter 2015).

Gender performance also seems to be involved when men consumed balut, especially during social drinking sessions. Although balut is eaten by everyone in the Philippines, young and old, men and women, when it comes to the practice of eating balut for its aphrodisiac properties, the performance of masculinity can be seen as it is asserted and confirmed with each act of consuming balut as an aphrodisiac for men only. In these contexts, males perform gender when eating fetal duck eggs specifically as an energizer to improve their sex life. During such occasions, the division is clear and seems designed to ensure that women are not eating it for their own enjoyment. Only for nutrition, and never as a stimulant. In this way, the act of consumption illustrates that gender is the product of interaction (West and Zimmerman 1987:129).

The belief that certain foods can lead to a more heightened state of arousal has led to a proliferation of foods considered as aphrodisiacs. Balut's reputation as a sexual energizer and stimulant for Filipino males has resulted in it being called a "natural" or "Filipino Viagra" by study participants. Arme Nicholas advertises her balut in farmers' markets in this way. Other distributors such as Cayetano Araujo use this idea as a marketing tool to sell balut to customers from other ethnicities.

Seven out of 26 study participants connected balut to the enhancement of the male's sexual experience, confirming the popular saying in Tagalog, "*pangpatigas ng tuhod*" (literally, strengthens the knee) as balut prolongs sex.

In the comments of the seven participants and the prevalent cultural belief, balut is indicated as an aphrodisiac.

## A short summary of aphrodisiacs

The earliest aphrodisiacs were inscribed on Babylonian tablets in 800 BCE (Benedek 1972) and the list of items considered as such is plentiful and includes birds' brains, bull testicles and donkey penises, shark fins and oysters, fruits like avocado and figs, and eggs. The more rare an edible substance, the more it may be seen as an aphrodisiac (Benedek 1972:7).

The connection of food and sex can be seen in the folk speech that contain names of food that can also have sexual meanings or erotolabia. These terms include "cherry," "nuts," "wiener," and other words that are "proof of man's universal preoccupation with the erotic character of foods" (Frazier 1970:8–9). Common phrases like "you look delicious" or "good enough to eat" or terms like "sweetie pie" and "honey" are a few more examples (Benedek 1972:10).

Eggs in particular have long been linked to sex and have been considered as aphrodisiacs for centuries. In the classic love manual *The Perfumed Garden* written 1394 BCE by Sheikh Nefzawi and translated by Sir Richard Burton in 1886, eggs are key for stimulating erections.

> He who will eat everyday, after fasting, the yolks of several eggs, will find in this aliment an energetic stimulant of the sexual powers … he who will feed for several days on eggs cooked with myrrh, cinnamon and pepper, will find an increased vigour in his erections and in his capacity for coition. His member will be in such a turgid state that it will seem as if it could never return to a state of repose. (Burton [1886] Burton and Arbuthnot 1988:154)

Nefzawi also mentions other recipes including eggs with honey and asparagus, both aphrodisiacs in their own right. Recipes from the Greeks, Romans, and the Chinese also mention eggs combined with other substances to magnify the eggs' purported aphrodisiac effects. Eggs symbolize fertility and the male testicles in countries like Germany, Ghana, and the Netherlands as well as in North and South America. In Morocco, Indonesia, and France, eggs represent the female hymen (Hendrickson 1974), while in the West, eggs have "feminine associations" (Jones 2005:139). Eggs are thought to give fertility to women while also promoting male virility (Newall 1971:113–141). Balut's very existence as a fertilized egg, a product of the mating of a drake and a female duck, is a potent reminder of virility and fecundity.

Eggs as representations of male testicles can also be seen in Philippine folk speech. It is not uncommon to hear Filipino men sometimes refer to their testicles as "*itlog*" (eggs) when speaking to their *barkada*. But this equation of eggs to testicles may not be the sole reason why balut is regarded as an aphrodisiac.

Just as some foods suggest sexual organs by their shape including asparagus, bananas, cucumber, figs, and avocados (see Benedek 1972; Frazier 1970; Goodland 1931; Walton 1958; Yoon 2006), there are foods whose manner of eating as well as shape may connote sex to the eater. Balut is one such example, and so are oysters which need to be eaten with a sucking-type of ingestion. Both foods are considered aphrodisiacs par excellence. Oysters, like other bivalves such as mussels and clams, contain the amino acid, D-Aspartic acid, which raised the sex hormones in experiments featuring lab rats (Ault 2017). Balut's nutritional breakdown includes 13.7 grams of protein per embryonated egg (see Table 1). Protein provides one with energy and stamina, effects that are sought in aphrodisiacs.

## Theoretical interpretations on orality

Renner in his work, *The Origin of Food Habits*, discusses the pleasurable aspects that people experience during the act of eating (1944). He writes that in addition to fulfilling hunger, the mouth, and most especially the lips where food passes through, have undeniable "sexual functions" (1944:64). Renner notes that to properly study the possible linkages of food to sex, the mouth must be included. Just as sensations like taste and smell cannot always be considered separately, it may be the same for "the two great impulses of food and sex" (Renner 1944:64–65). Renner argues that deep in our food habits can lurk unconscious and meaningful phenomena.

The connections between food and sex are constantly alluded to in many a magazine, a television show, or a film. This is demonstrated by one of the most popular episodes of Anthony Bourdain's *No Reservations* which was titled "Food Porn" in Season 5, Episode 7 which was followed up by another episode titled "Food Porn 2" in Season 6, Episode 10.

Renner continues to explore this psychoanalytical view by pointing out that for Freud, "the sucking of the infant is the first sexual act of a human being. It is believed that this sexual pleasure is first bound up with the action of feeding at the mother's breast but that the child soon learns to separate this pleasure, so that later on when the child is weaned the pleasure becomes transferred to parts of his own body such as the thumb and the tongue … this is called autoeroticism, and the lips erogenous zones" (1944:65).

Even when the child grows up to an adult, and he or she has to forsake sucking which can be noisy as prim and proper behavior is demanded by social etiquette, the adult in effect still "sucks" when sipping liquids. To sip a drink like wine or tea not only enhances the experience of taste but it is also an act reminiscent of the unconscious sexual pleasure of sucking. For Renner, "the sipping of liquids has almost always some connection with the pleasure of sucking for its own sake … the sipping of liquids by grown-ups bears a very close relation to sucking, as do also the many existing varieties of smoking" (1944:70).[3]

The physical sensations one obtains from eating illustrate that the relationship of food and sex goes beyond psychological considerations. Our taste-buds and certain areas of our body such as the clitoris and lips are sensitive to stimulation. "Man's urge to engage in oral-genital act is as natural and healthy as his desire to partake of tasty and satisfying foods" (Frazier 1970:9).

Gershon Legman is a folklorist who wrote about oragenitalism and the cultural practices associated with it (1969). Oragenital acts "are not essentially a special type of sex technique, intended to satisfy the erotic needs of the genital partner, but are the expression of a profound psychological urge, and intended to satisfy the erotic needs of the oral partner" (Legman 1969:13). Legman points out that sexual folklore on cunnilinctus recognizes the oral desires of those men wishing to perform oral sex on women. He gives the example of tales featuring "dying men asking the nurse to let them perform cunnilinctus—which they have sworn to try once before they die—and invariably being revived by it … even made immortal, as though they had drunk, in this way, at the maternal Fountain of Life" (1969:14).

He emphasizes that like fellation, cunnilinctus should be studied with the realization that the motivation of the act comes from "oral and even masochistic strivings—the desire to return to the mother's breast, or frankly to her womb, and certainly to infant independence," and as such the motivation is more important than the desire to excite the genital partner with this technique (1969:14).

Legman admits that one should not forget that the woman who is being caressed in this manner feels pleasure as well, but he stresses that cunnilinctus "is surely as much as the Freudian return to the womb, as to the maternal breast, with all the emotional power of these symbols and these realities" (1969:15). In reaching this conclusion, Legman makes his argument particularly striking by alluding to the fact that with the exception of Caesarean and breech births, "every human life begins … with the act of cunnilinctus performed by the infant at birth, over the whole length of the mother's vagina, from the inside out!" (1969:15).

Although not everyone may agree with Legman regarding oragenitalism motivation, what is relevant to this balut study is the idea that sucking is an essential and common method used by a person performing this oral act (Legman 1969:51). If there is unconscious sexual pleasure derived from the actions of sipping and sucking, this may be another reason why balut is an aphrodisiac because the method of eating it may suggest to some an association with oral sex.

I should stress here that not everyone associates the process of cracking the tip of the balut egg, boring a small hole, and sucking its juice—the most common method of consuming the egg—to be related to sex. It is, after all, a necessity to drink the juice when eating the egg if one does not want to dribble juice all over oneself. But if eaten as an aphrodisiac, one may see the sensual imagery of sucking out the juice from the egg.

## Linguistic terms and some possible suggestions of balut-eating

It should be emphasized that none of my study participants described eating balut as a sexual act. I examine, instead, their linguistic use of terms as evidence that points to the possible connections between balut-eating and the reasons why it is seen as an aphrodisiac. When describing their methods of drinking the liquid inside the balut, study participants used the words sip, suck, and drink. The word "sip" was the most popular word, and the closest word to it in Tagalog is "*sipsip*," which was used by several of my informants when they talked to me in that language.

The word "*sipsip*" does not exactly translate to mean "sip"; instead, it means more like the word "suck." As such, "*sipsip*" or the object focus form of the word, "*sipsipin*," is often imbued with a negative connotation. Although *sipsip* means to sip or suck liquids, its colloquial meaning is "a person who toadies to authority," a meaning that is particularly relevant in light of past and present political situations in the Philippines (Fernandez and Alegre 1988:88). In other words, a "*sipsip*" is a sycophant who curries favor and ingratiates himself to people with power or who are rich. One could even say that a "*sipsip*" is like a leech in the way he or she "sucks" up to people. With these definitions, therefore, one can consider the Tagalog word "*sipsip*" as one more piece of evidence relating the word sip to the word suck, a linguistic and cultural connection which goes beyond Renner's point that was limited to the way one eats.

The balut-eater typically sips or sucks the liquid through the small hole in the egg before eating the rest of the parts. Called "sabaw" or the soup, the balut consumer is in effect drinking the amniotic liquid from the egg, from the hole created. Males who eat balut are eating what is literally a chick and drinking its fluids. In addition, I suggest that in light of the folklore surrounding the egg that was noted above, it can be interpreted that when the male balut-eater first cracks the egg and makes a small hole for the juice, he can be seen as symbolically breaking the woman's hymen.

Women are sometimes called "chicks" in the Philippines and many other countries like the United States. Describing the folk art in the highly decorated jeepneys in Manila, Menez observes that the "CHICKSeater" inscribed on the vehicle can be translated to refer to the driver eating balut or that the "chicks" can also be presumed to mean "girls" (Menez 1996:6). If the latter meaning is intended, it could be also interpreted as the driver boasting about his sexual prowess. This objectification of women as parts of an animal to be consumed is part of the male domination script (Calvert 2014). Many men eat eggs as well as drink milk to build their strength and may be illustrating a "symbolic domination over women and their reproductive capacity" (Jones 2005:139, paraphrasing Heisley 1990:9).

A common theme raised by study respondents is that many avoided looking at the embryo inside the balut. Many of them prefer to swallow the balut in two to three bites rather than risk seeing it. This suggests a fear of the embryo's appearance. Sexual folklore suggests that some men do not like to look at the vagina while in the process of "eating" it. Numerous jokes abound regarding the scariness of a vagina's looks, and this perception of the vagina as a monster or something to be afraid of is well documented in the widespread phenomena of *vagina dentata* (Otero 1996; Latin term for "toothed vagina").

Beit-Hallahmi writes that just as men are attracted to the vagina, they are also repulsed by it. "The explanations may be found at both psychological and social levels … such beliefs reflect fear of women and fear of genitals. At the social level they reflect a generally negative attitude towards women" (1985:351).

The fear of the embryo may not just be related to the concept of vagina dentata, but it may also express the folks' unconscious association of the balut embryo with that of the human fetus. A few study participants, mostly females, noted they do not like eating the embryo in balut.

## Why only for men? Performing masculinity

None of the study participants interviewed or who responded to the online survey discussed the aphrodisiac effects of balut for women. If stating balut as an aphrodisiac, participants only mentioned that it was good for the male, not the female. Yes, balut was eaten by women and children and even the sick to provide energy and nutrition but when eaten as an aphrodisiac, it was only good for the man. The man who eats balut gets "strong knees" and is able to function sexually. There is no mention about what women can get sexually from eating balut.

Once again, the arrival of the Spanish conquistadors offers a clue to how this idea that balut's reputed effects as an aphrodisiac benefits only the male. Along with Christianity, the Spanish also brought their own ideas of sexuality and masculinity that they attempted to impart to the indigenous tribes. Describing the natives' sexual traditions at the time of Spanish contact, historian Antonio de Morga wrote in the seventeenth century that there were men "whose business was to ravish and take away the virginity of girls. These girls were taken to such men, and the latter were paid for ravishing them, for the natives considered it a hindrance and impediment if the girls were virgins when married" (as cited in Garcia 1979:303).

Further evidence that the indigenous women had their own ideas of sexuality may be drawn from the Spanish chroniclers' description of a metal or ivory bolt that was inserted at the tip of a Filipino man's penis, as part of the custom that was meant for the sexual enjoyment of women. Although it inflicted pain and discomfort, Filipino males insisted that such a device must be worn, according to Pigafetta. "They say that their women wish it so, and that if they did otherwise they would not have communication with them" (Pigafetta as cited in Jocano 1975a: 67; also see De Morga as cited in Garcia 1979:303).

In the belief that balut is good sexually only for men, such gendered notions continue to reproduce a specific idea of masculinity which discriminates against different forms of masculinities (and femininities). The cultural acceptance of "machismo" that was propagated by the Spanish can shed light on such limited ideas of sexuality. In Tomas Andres's *Dictionary of Filipino Culture and Values*, machismo is defined as a "belief in male supremacy and the relegation of the women to a domestic role and as second-class citizens" (1994:97).

In an earlier work, Andres clarifies the extent machismo is ingrained in Philippine society, despite the respect that mothers and other matriarchal figures command (Andres 1987). Andres blames machismo for influencing Filipino males, poor and rich alike "to engage in a sexual role which could only be verified by the peer group to which he belongs in terms of the number of affairs he maintains and children he sires either with his lawful wife or his mistresses" (1987:4).

A double standard exists where women are expected to be chaste and faithful while men are not upheld to the same standards and are instead, spurred on to have "queridas" or mistresses while being married. In spite of her husband's culturally sanctioned philandering, a wife "is required strict and persevering fidelity and chastity ... acclaimed as virtuous if she suffers martyrdom and keeps her chastity for the unfaithful husband to come home" (Andres 1987:5). Andres names factors that make it easy for Filipino males to be unfaithful, including the tropical hot weather, drinking or *inuman*, and the "abundance of spicy food and aphrodisiacs," all of which combine to drive men to have queridas and be the father of as many first-born children as they can (1987:7).

This idea of hyper masculinity continues to have currency with an estimated 21 percent of married Filipino men engaging in extramarital affairs, according to national statistics taken in 2003 (Abalos 2011). On the flip side of this exaggerated masculinity is the obsession with the hymen. "By embedding in the consciousness of women from early childhood the belief that the hymen—or what it symbolizes, virginity—is crucial to the maidenhood and self-esteem, Philippine society predetermines the woman's sense of well-being and personal fulfillment to one validating male supremacy or dominance" (Azurin 1995:157). The cultural emphasis on the value of the hymen has led to "female masochism—as manifested in the perennially pregnant but emaciated women, the periodically bruised and the ever-forgiving *abandonadas*" (Azurin 1995:163) who are portrayed in the culture, media like telenovelas, and literature as the long-suffering wives of philandering Filipino men.

The above interpretation of balut's connection to cultural beliefs, whether symbolic such as the *aswang* and Othering, or psychological such as an aphrodisiac exclusively for men, provide evidence of food's communicative powers in illuminating social relations, practices of inclusion and exclusion as well as cultural beliefs on sex. To interpret balut as only good for males would be to enforce the idea of women as objects without agency to perform their own sexuality. It also relegates men to a more rigid type of masculinity. By examining balut's connections to widespread cultural beliefs, it is my hope to make more room for the realization of other scripts or other possibilities of the self.

# Performing Identity through Balut-Eating Contests

Through the examination of what balut has come to represent for many Filipino Americans, it has become clear that it is now a food that validates a "true" Filipino from the rest, a source of comfort for many who are "culturally dislocated" in terms of both geographic distance from the motherland and alienated by the mainstream culture around them. In consuming the fertilized egg, the act of consumption also brings the pleasure of being in control of at least one action despite the external pressures away from home (see Appadurai 1996:7). The eater is given the choice or agency (whether illusion or not) to consume a fertilized egg, which upon consumption may result in successful identity-making in a public setting, as seen in the example of balut-eating contests below.

On a sunny afternoon in August 2017 in San Francisco, California, over the approving roar of the crowd competing with loud pop music played by Filipino musicians on a distant stage, emcee PJ Quesada counts down to the start of the final round of competitive balut-eating: two male contestants face off to eat three balut in less than five minutes. Tension mounts, the contestants get ready, and then they are off. Cracking the shells, sipping and munching, the end result when the winner is declared is a messy tangle of fragmented shells, spilled embryonic fluid on the table and a beaming winner, Romeo Perez, who takes off his hat bearing the Philippine flag to reveal yet another baseball cap emblazoned with the word "Champions." After inspecting the debris, which was minimal as Romeo had eaten the three eggs, including most of the shells with only one hand (his other arm was a prosthetic), PJ the emcee lifts Romeo's hand in victory and declares him the winner, for the seventh time in the last seven years.

A similar scene unfolds each October in the Speedy Balut ® Contest as part of the Fil-Am Heritage annual celebration in Maui, Hawai'i. An online video of the event in 2013 shows a group of experienced balut-eaters rapidly eating balut to the tune of the Black-Eyed Pea's hit song "Bebot," while its chorus of "Fi-li-pi-no" resonated in the background. Unlike the Pistahan contest which allows everyone to join, however, the Maui contest welcomes only contestants who are practiced balut consumers. In its choice of music, contest rules, and of course the food itself, the balut contest in Maui is palpably nationalistic compared to the less obvious, but still noticeably patriotic, San Francisco contest.

The largest of all the balut-eating contests was the New York contest that was sponsored by the popular Jeepney and Maharlika Filipino restaurants. With a format that draws inspiration from Nathan's Famous Hot Dog-eating contest held annually in Coney Island, the winner was the one who ate the most balut in a short amount of time. Filipino American Wayne Algenio won the first contest in 2012 ingesting 18 eggs, followed by 27 eggs in 2013, and in 2014, he ate 13 more balut than the year before (Figure 16).

Eating contests have long been a familiar standby in American fairs, with Nathan's Famous Hot Dog-eating contest dating back to 1916 according to some accounts (see Halloran 2004). Older than the Nathan's contest is that of a pie-eating competition, with the first written account of such an event occurring in 1878 (Lohman 2016). For these balut contests, however, apple pies and hot dogs were not on the menu. Instead, as its name states, balut-eating contests highlight the eating of fetal duck eggs, a more recent entry to the competitive eating field.

From the shores of Maui, Hawai'i to those of the New York coast, balut-eating contests are occurring regularly during Asian American festivals and Filipino American heritage celebrations. Although the New York contest has since been discontinued, a New Jersey one has appeared beginning in 2015. These contests are usually the main attraction of the festivals and are typically filmed and uploaded on the internet to be watched by an online audience. What is the purpose of such contests and why are they being held? What is being communicated in the consumption of balut during these competitive eating events? Using ethnographic data from my fieldwork observing two balut-eating contests in San Francisco in 2016 and 2017, interviews with

**Figure 16** Wayne Algenio, competitive eating champion at 2013 balut-eating contest in New York—Courtesy of Wayne Algenio.

participants and observations of videos featuring balut-eating contests and analysis of media discourse, I argue how such events illustrate how food can be both democratic and a source of status and distinction (Bourdieu [1979] 1984; Johnston and Baumann 2010).

Such events can also typify culinary tourism, which is defined "as the intentional, exploratory participation in the foodways of an other" (Long

2004:21). Balut has become a tourist attraction in its own right, and travel is not needed for people to feel that they have gone to Southeast Asia by watching others ingest such a delicacy (Long 2004:11). But the contests signify more than tourism. The issues of belonging and nationalism also bring people to watch and participate in balut contests and these events offer the chance for many to be part of a group that normally has been seen but not heard.

Balut contests and similar ones illustrate how foods can be used to produce a national identity. "Foodstuffs and eating are a way to negotiate national interests or perhaps more accurately, a way to establish what it means to be part of a group—a relapsing into 19th century ways of thinking under the aegis of 21st century competitive rivalries and dynamics" (Bendix and Fenske 2014:17). Eating and competing against others during the balut contest enable one to lay claim to being "Filipino," to belong to that group, even if it was only for that limited moment of consumption.

Establishing oneself as part of a group of members who claim "Filipino-ness" via a rivalry involving the eating of balut is evident when I interviewed the three-time winner of the New York balut contest, Wayne Algenio. Although Wayne tells me that he doesn't mind losing to someone who isn't Filipino, pride is evident in his voice when he describes himself as "an ambassador of balut." He confesses that he felt more pressure to win by the time he participated in the 2014 contest. At that time, his two closest competitors were a Filipino man he called "*Tito*" (uncle) and a male participant of Chinese heritage, who were each able to eat 34 eggs while Wayne downed 40 balut. Wayne felt more inclined to lose to "Tito," but not to the other competitor. His winning cemented his status as a Filipino American in the community and also established his identity as a "patriot" in the eyes of other Filipino Americans.

In addition, by ingesting a widely reviled food such as balut in a competition, participants (and organizers) of such events utilize this food as a way to gain citizenship in the greater sociocultural landscape as foodies (Johnston and Baumann 2010) who are able to wield culinary capital. As Naccarato and Lebesco (2012) have shown, obtaining culinary capital can emerge from paradoxical food practices whether stemming from the ·linary elite or from the "everyman" consumption of "junk food" in fairs and festivals. Status is conferred to those who can make or eat a food that is considered by the mainstream as the very best or, in the case of balut, the worse kind of food. In the eating of such a food (or other foods considered as "repulsive" by many such as fish eyeballs, bull's testicles, or maggot-laced cheese), the consumer is proven to be open to a wide-ranging breadth of food experiences and thus is recognized by others as having the most cultural capital through culinary means (Naccarato and Lebesco 2012). More often than not, this culinary capital can be turned by foodies into real economic gain as will be soon illustrated.

The contests can also be seen as part of a localized genre, with similar features to the "racial eating contest" (Vardi 2010) of the early twentieth century which featured African Americans in gorging competitions as a source of amusement for whites interested in further delineating themselves from the Other. Rather than categorizing balut-eating contests as events that further emphasize the difference, however, such events provide Filipino Americans pleasure and agency to propagate selected cultural practices and defy the conventional stigmatism of their culture and cuisine.

Using the framework of the eating contest as a communicative practice that consists of "artistic communication between small groups" (Ben-Amos 1971), balut-eating contests can be seen as a practice that communicates issues of "ethnic" identity and also confers culinary capital to participants. The balut-eaters conduct the communication between themselves and the audience. Their eating practice may not fall in the general understanding of "artistic" communication, but there is indeed a method of consuming during a contest that is a form of communication that can garner approval from the audience. It is an "artistic communication" in that it requires certain skills and finesse in order to be the "best" balut-eater in the contest.

Such contests may also illustrate what Alan Dundes coined as "metafolklore" and further expanded on by Ben-Amos "to mean the conception a culture has of its own folkloric communication ... and the sense of the social appropriateness of their application in various cultural situations" (Ben-Amos 1976:226). Whether consuming an insider food like balut in a highly public setting, or surrounding such contests in nationalist discourse, it is apparent that many Filipino Americans are using the balut contests to negotiate what it means to be of Filipino heritage in present-day United States.

# The festival frame

Out of the five balut-eating contests that I examined, four took place within the festival frame, except for the New York contest which occurred at a street fair. This led me to consider the nature of a festival and its characteristics. Much has been written on festivals by folklorists[1], but of particular relevance is Alessandro Falassi's 1987 edited volume on festivals. As a genre of folklore, festivals refer to a time when a community bound by similar interests and worldview behave in a way that is not usual; instead, "they carry to the extreme behaviors that are usually regulated by measure; they invert patterns of daily social life" (Falassi 1987:3). Festivals usually incorporate rites-of-passage where one is initiated either in a specific age group or some other group.[2] The rites also include "rites of conspicuous consumption" where food and drink play a major part (Falassi 1987:4).

A festival has moments that have been described by scholar Roger Abrahams as "festive times-out-of-time of orgy, of bacchanal, of Carnival" where one is inclined to be "equal opportunity eaters," especially in situations where one can taste strange food and drink strange brews to the point of "losing oneself" (Abrahams 1984:19). Balut-eating contests which take place during Asian and Filipino festivals in America are events held by the Filipino American community in a special period "time out of time" where eating balut rapidly and in huge quantities can be labeled "extreme" by some. These characteristics in a balut-eating contest fall under the general definition of a festival, where contestants are inclined to try new and strange things that they may not even consider during ordinary time.

The concept of *communitas* or Latin for community as espoused by Victor Turner is of interest for this study (Turner 1967). *Communitas* can be described as a feeling of becoming a member of a group where everyone is on the same level and sharing commonalities with each other. Turner notes that *communitas* happens during festivals, during a period "in and out of time" that is liminal[3] where society is unstructured and where social life emerges in a form of *communitas* and individuals are more equals (Turner 1967:360). *Communitas* describes the spirit of a community whose members are all peers and equals, but it is a fleeting momentum. The kind of *communitas* that is relevant here is a "spontaneous communitas," that although temporary, once it seizes the group, there is a "high value in personal honesty, openness, and lack of pretensions or pretentiousness" (Turner 1974:79).[4]

Such *communitas* is evident in the Pistahan festival which has taken place for over 26 years in the Yerba Buena Gardens, located in the heart of San Francisco, California. Billed in its Facebook page as the "largest celebration of Filipino art, dance, music and food," the festival draws thousands of attendants with its promise of booths featuring arts, crafts, products, and performances of Filipino stars on the main stage.

This could be seen in the extemporaneous reception of the emcee PJ Quesada's monologue on balut used as a "tool of oppression" (see Chapter 2). As a participant-observer in the crowd, I was struck with a "magical" sense of communal understanding during that here-and-now moment. It was as if the moment allowed a glimpse of what could be, that all the indignities and past inequalities could be forgotten and we in the crowd had the power to make it so (see Turner 1974:79). It was beyond the usual entertainment of an "eating" contest. The raw openness of PJ's monologue was welcomed by the crowd who had become aware of their similarities in their backgrounds as Filipino Americans. They urged him in their reactions to continue to cultivate that moment of belonging.

It may be said that overall, the Pistahan festival itself had these moments of *communitas*, assisted with the ever-present background of food which lent its power to absorb festival-goers in a moment of synchronicity where participants felt connected and equal with others. The flashes of communal understanding would not have been possible without it. Breaking bread, or in this instance, breaking the balut shell brought on this *communitas*. It was a demonstration of food's ability to bring (and keep) people together, uniting members and solidifying the relationship so that participants return to the festival each year expending time and money to attend (see Kalcik 1984). The competitive aspect of the contest also draws individuals in and contributes to the delineation of the group's boundaries.

Whether it was Filipino-style barbecues, *lumpia* or *pansit*, the unabashed celebration of balut or the overall revelry, all these components of the festival lured me and others to "lose ourselves" in eating and drinking. The Pistahan festival was thus the perfect place to hold an eating contest. Indeed, there were several featured contests, including ice cream- and vinegar-tasting competitions, of which I participated in (and failed miserably).

But it was the balut-eating contest that drew the most notice. As a main attraction, the format of the balut-eating contest consisted of a preliminary round with two to three balut. In the final round, up to five balut may have to be eaten. The prizes were gift certificates in the amount of $100 for the first place, $75 for placing second place, and $50 for coming in third.

## "New" tradition bearers

Watching the elimination rounds which boiled down to the last two contestants in the 2017 Pistahan contest, I noted that several of the contestants were returning competitors from 2016. Participants in the final round consisted of Romeo Perez, who had won the contest for the past six years, and a new challenger from the local Philippine embassy. Both men had survived the winnowing of the original 33 eager contestants who had signed up to eat one balut. They had eaten at least six balut to get to the last round of three. The prize was ostensibly $100 but judging from participants' comments, money was not the only lure.

It is the act of eating balut itself that was the real prize as well. Participants used the contest to consume a food that is not always easy to procure despite its availability in specialty stores and select restaurants. Although widely available in the Philippines for the equivalent of 33 cents or less, balut in the United States are sold more than triple the price in farmer's markets and 12 times greater in restaurants in New York. Once in the United States, balut has effectively been transformed to a high-value food, placing it out of reach for some groups of people. This is fitting with its status as an "exotic" and "authentic" food in the Western world that can be used as a source of differentiation and distinction (Johnston and Baumann 2010).

At 12, Matthew Layag was the youngest participant in the 2016 Pistahan balut-eating contest (Figure 17). When asked why he joined, Matthew explains the following: "Because I like balut and I wanted to have some. The only reason I joined was so I could have free balut." According to Matthew's father Nelson Layag, although he himself does not eat balut, seeing his son Matthew enjoy it in the contest "was awesome ... I have been very intentional and passionate about making sure my children know their Filipino roots." In fact, now that

**Figure 17** Twelve-year-old Matthew Layag tries his hand at the balut-eating contest with Romeo Perez.

he has witnessed Matthew eating balut and liking it, Nelson states he would "maybe" try it again.

Romeo Perez, the seven-time Pistahan champion, is a Filipino American who shared with me that he only eats balut during the yearly competitions. He was familiar with them before the contest but does not consume balut regularly when he is not in competition. For Wayne Algenio, the New York winner, the first time he ate balut was during the 2012 competition. Although Wayne does not eat balut in everyday life, he promotes it where he can. Despite only indulging in the cultural practice on occasion, it can be argued that all three are tradition makers, ensuring that the expressive practice of eating balut is known and continued whether occasionally or more often (Figure 18). Wayne, Romeo, and even Matthew at a young age can be viewed as "active bearers" of the lore (eating balut) in that they are exposing others to the cultural practice of eating balut while within the frame of an eating contest. Others who can also belong to this group is Arme Nicholas (Chapter 1) who initiated customers

**Figure 18** Semi-finals at 2016 balut-eating contest. From left to right, Matthew Layag, Romeo Perez, Marlon Macaida, and Sergio Reyes Raya.

who shop at her stall at the farmer's markets and PJ Quesada, emcee of the contest. An active bearer was defined by Swedish folklorist Carl Wilhelm Sydow to mean those individuals who can transmit a tradition (Sydow [1948] 1977).[5] That is to say, the active bearer is a person who is knowledgeable about a cultural practice and can teach others how to do it.

The performances of Wayne, Matthew, and Romeo live on in various websites such as YouTube, ensuring that others are exposed to this expressive culture for years to come. They can also teach others in a face-to-face manner. All three can effectively communicate and transmit the "lore" of eating balut, ranging from techniques for consuming the embryonic egg, to cultural appreciation for this delicacy and its connection to Filipino identity.

Through his cultural knowledge of how to eat balut and his understanding of its importance to being a Filipino American and his appreciation for the nuances of its taste, Matthew is especially poised to be a tradition bearer in the sense that despite his young age, he can teach others the proper cultural context and skills to consume it. His developed palate at a young age and his exposure to the cultural practice of eating balut via eating contests has made Matthew an example of how knowledge can be transmitted in various ways, such as digitally, in this age of the internet. The long-standing images of wizened folks who teach the youth to carry on ancient traditions have been indelibly stamped in the minds of many. The reality is, however, that with technology, that image has to be flipped: "We might instead conceive of digital culture fostering a *handing up* of vernacular knowledge by young, wired wizards with mythic imagination and social ebullience" (Bronner 2009:32).

Balut-eating contests can be viewed as a successful hybrid that entertains as well as educates, a combination that some contest organizers like Tita Pearl Parmelee strive to do. Called "Festival Queen," Tita Pearl is a well-known figure in the Filipino community in the San Francisco Bay Area and she is one of the primary organizers and volunteers for Pistahan. Tita Pearl is also a director of the Filipino Food Movement, a non profit organization that was the brainchild of PJ Quesada whose family owns and operates Ramar Foods, the largest manufacturer of Filipino foods in the United States. The Filipino Food Movement aims to promote Filipino culture and cuisine.

Born and raised in Palawan, Philippines, Tita Pearl came to the United States in 1976. As a promoter of Philippine products, she traveled around the country visiting church fairs and festivals big and small. She took events like *adobo* cook-offs and balut-eating contests and marketed them throughout Filipino communities in the United States. Besides Pistahan, she has also volunteered for two decades at the Festival of Philippine Arts and Culture (FPAC) in Los Angeles, billed as the biggest gathering for Filipino arts and culture in southern California. The FPAC also features a balut-eating festival as one of its main attractions.

I watched Tita Peal in action during the balut-eating contests held in 2016 and 2017. She proved to be a whirl of activity as she gathered contestants, gave out prizes, and enforced the rules as the contests unfolded.

## "Keying" the contest

Before the actual contest is held, a volunteer is plucked from the audience to demonstrate how to eat balut. "It's to make the contest hot," notes Tita P

"I have one person taste it for the first time, and tell the audience what is balut, like a story." Making the contest "hot" is to increase the attraction of the contest by making it resemble reality television in its beginning moments, to prime the audience by using the controversial power of balut and its "disgusting" reputation. The volunteer's experience complete with his or her struggles to consume the egg and overcome cultural bias frames the eating contest and enables the audience members to anticipate the events to come. All the balut contests I watched live or online employed the interactive device of inviting the audience to participate by eating the fetal egg.

During the 2017 Pistahan, the preliminary performance to the actual balut-eating contest was initiated when a novice balut-eater was selected from the audience. An African American male volunteered. After listening to a short explanation of what is balut, the time came for him to try it. Consuming the egg was clearly a challenge. Each time he grimaced or winced, the build up of anticipation from the audience could be palpably felt.

Although the volunteer may not have thought that his actions were a type of performance, his gestures and facial expressions which spoke volumes served as a "'keying' of performance" (Bauman 1974:295). His performance sets up a frame, within which "the messages being communicated are to be understood" (Bauman 1974:292).

The contorted expressions, shaking of the head, and the gagging motions that are eventually overcome, albeit temporarily, when the volunteer swallows the balut—all are features that have become part of the conventional performance of disgust that has been highlighted in Western television and video blogs. Although the 2017 volunteer was game and up for a challenge, his reactions when eating the egg were indicative how disgust can be a product of culture and nurture, despite also being common to the human species (Jones 2000:55).

In addition to consuming balut, the volunteer balut-eater was asked to describe the taste and texture. His description in the form of a personal narrative served to elicit empathy. By performing appropriately or as expected by the audience, the volunteer eater was able to express the sensory aspects of eating balut—allowing the audience to imagine how he felt when confronted with the feathery texture and the formed chick, the taste and smell of the balut. Since the eating of the balut was clearly not something he did for nourishment, but for entertainment, the novice balut-eater was demonstrating the process of when "food events move towards the theatrical, and, more specifically, towards the spectacular" (Kirshenblatt-Gimblett 1999:2). In addition, the novice balut-eater displayed competence in his performance as it enhanced the anticipatory mood and experience of the audience, who rewarded him with loud applause and admiration.

In Tita Pearl's mind, balut has undoubtedly expanded the awareness of people about Filipino cuisine. She fields many a call from people who ask her where to buy it and how to prepare it. But there is also a lot of negative attention from others who call and let her know their disapproval. According to Tita Pearl, some of the comments include "Why do you do that?" and "You should just let the embryo grow."

Referring to the ubiquitous presence of balut in the landscape of the Philippines, Tita Pearl wishes that people were more open-minded about balut and Filipino culture. "For us, balut is ordinary … it's our culture." In the end, she considers all the remarks, bad or good, as a positive thing. "For me, it's part of my culture that I have to accept," Tita Pearl remarks. "Because that means they are paying attention. They are curious."

Her remarks offer a clue to balut's drawing power. Balut's reputation as a "Franken-snack" as it was described in the *New York Times* (Vadukul 2012) is exactly what lures the curious who have been initiated into the balut-as-object-of-disgust stereotype via reality shows or social media.

Not surprisingly, the idea for Pistahan's balut-eating contest, which marked its 16th year of existence in 2018, owes its existence to the infamous reality television episode featuring balut in 2002. Tita Pearl conceived the idea for the contest when she watched the show:

> People will come because of *Fear Factor* and curiosity. I wanted to be shocked … I don't eat balut. I do not … It kind of scares me, so I have to face my fear. You remember the good things, and you remember the things that scare you or things that are unusual.

According to Tita Pearl, in the early days of the contest, there were a few takers, but that has changed the last five years when a limit was placed on the number of participants. Its popularity can be gauged by the number of participants who signed up. In 2016, there were a total of eight people and in 2017, over 30 individuals turned up at the festival booth to consume balut. This prompted several elimination rounds to fit everyone who wanted to compete.

Both the curiosity factor and the rising popularity of Filipino food may have enticed a huge crowd in the 2017 Pistahan balut contest, with standing-room only and no empty seats (Figure 19). The balut contest gathered the most number of curious watchers, more than the ice cream-tasting test, the polvoron (*powder*) candy- and vinegar-tasting contest which all took place in the culinary pavilion. I estimated the crowd to be over a hundred spectators, all gazing collectively at the spectacle about to unfold. Depending on the stage of the contest, people came and went during the preparation of the balut (Figure 20), but many stayed to watch the winner announced (Figure 21). By the time clean up of the contest debris was being done (Figure 22), the crowd had dissipated.

The anticipatory "gazing" can be seen as an example of what sociologist John Urry had described as the tourist gaze, which is socially constructed and differs

**Figure 19** Crowd gathers to watch the 2017 balut-eating contest in San Francisco, California.

**Figure 20** Balut eggs being prepared for the 2017 Pistahan festival's balut-eating contest.

according to the group, society, or history (Urry [1990] 2002:1). Of particular relevance here is the "collective gaze" that involves "conviviality" which results in a sense of carnival (Urry [1990] 2002:150). With the large numbers of people present, the collective gaze was evident during the Pistahan's contest, implying that the balut-eating site was **the** place to be for many.

The balut contest had effectively become a tourist attraction, where "intense pleasure" was derived from the anticipation of the contest, generated and sustained by numerous television shows and online videos which created the tourist gaze at balut (see Urry [1990] 2002:3).

**Figure 21** PJ Quesada of the Filipino Food Movement congratulates Romeo Perez, the winner of the 2017 balut-eating contest.

**Figure 22** The detritus of the 2016 balut-eating contest.

As I attempted to watch the proceedings, however, I was elbowed by a 60-something white woman with an expression of loathing on her face. She stood with her arms crossed, her face appalled, revolted, and fascinated at the same time. Her reaction aligned with those of the New York crowd in 2014, when Jeepney co-owner Nicole Ponseca described in an interview with NBC News that people's response was "a combination of awe, audacity, and borderline grossed out." Her gaze was neither romantic nor collective but instead can be characterized as a racialized gaze that resulted in a non-communitas with others.

## Competitive eaters of balut

The balut-eating contest drew prospective contestants from all walks of life. Some of them were more experienced in the realm of competitive eating. To understand how participants in balut-eating contests are motivated and how their actions may garner culinary capital, I interviewed two of them in depth. As mentioned before, Wayne Algenio is a competitive eater champion who has been featured in international and national news for winning the balut-eating contests in New York. He also is now known for his feat of consuming 22 hot chilies or Carolina Reapers in one minute. For this latter achievement, Wayne broke the Guinness World record. I met Wayne through a contact who had interviewed him for a magazine article. With that introduction, I interviewed Wayne by phone in 2015 and 2016.

Born in Queens, New York in 1984, Wayne's father is from the Quezon Province and his mother is from Vigan, Philippines. Although he has gone on to win other food contests, Wayne admits that winning the balut contest three years in a row has given him more visibility than any other contest, with the exception of breaking the Guinness World Record in 2016 for eating the most number of Carolina Reapers in one minute. "That [balut] contest definitely gave me the most recognition than any other contest," Wayne says. "The social media aspect alone is probably bigger than any contest I've done."

For eating balut, Wayne was featured in the Filipino television channel, and quoted in newspapers from New York to the Philippines. He was in the internationally circulated *Asian Journal* and featured in *Ripley's Believe It or* triple-winning feat of eating the greatest number of balut under

When asked about why he thinks there was so much publicity and social media buzz surrounding balut-eating contests, Wayne has a ready answer.

"Because of the food itself," Wayne states. "It's a weird food, and they used that food in shows like *Fear Factor*. That's where most people recognized it from, I think. So it's one of those foods that's supposed to be scary to eat."

Even in the ultra competitive eating world, Wayne is known for his feats with balut. For mastering the performance of eating balut, and eating it well, the recognition came quick. "No one wants to touch this contest because they don't want to try balut," he says with a laugh. "Most of them don't want to try it for the fact that they think it's disgusting ... That's how they recognize me. So that's what they say when they first meet me, 'Oh, he's the guy who ate all that balut, I would never eat that.'" Even though there is a cash prize involved, Wayne contends that it is not enough to lure most competitive eaters to try balut.

Wayne's balut-eating prowess has even made his reputation outside the competitive eating world:

> That's how I became known to other people. And even people from my own culture, it's been that around my friends, or acquaintances. I was getting notifications on Facebook, they tagged me, in the balut-eating contests. They saw pictures of me in social media. Or classmates I haven't seen in years. Everyone was just surprised that I ate that and I won.

Balut has become a sort of test for Wayne to determine if someone he meets would be open-minded enough and willing to try it. "Whenever I date someone, I always make them try balut," he says. "I tell them jokingly, 'you can't date the champion unless you eat one balut.'"

For Wayne, competitive eating is not about economic gain as he usually does not get cash or even use his gift cards. He says that he is attracted to the social aspect and making new friends. Wayne has his own YouTube channel, where he posts all the contests he has done. For Wayne, it is a video diary so he could look back when older to see all the "cool things" he has experienced.

The downside to this recognition is the vicious remarks that animal activists have left on his websites, and the exposure to online trolling. "When there's articles on Facebook, I will read the comments and people will say I'm disgusting and that's a horrible thing to do." The statements ranged from "Oh, that's cruel," to death threats. Wayne says he does not know what type of people leaves these comments and if they are against the whole balut-eating contest or the eating of baby ducks in general.

As a child in Queens, Wayne was exposed "half and half" to both the American and Filipino cultures. He learned to use the "tabo" (small bucket) to take his showers and ate rice for every meal. He grew up speaking English because his mother spoke the Ilocano dialect while his father was fluent in Tagalog, and English is the language they communicated with each other.

When asked if he feels more American or Filipino, Wayne chuckles, saying:

> I was a very confused kid … I was just trying to learn to be me. I can't really say I didn't feel as Filipino. I knew I was Filipino, but in the sense, of what really is a Filipino.

The first time he ever heard about balut was in 2012, the year of the first balut-eating contest sponsored by the gastro pub Jeepney and Maharlika restaurant. It was heavily advertised on social media but Wayne first found out about it in an eating contest website, Eatbeatss.com, which lists eating contests in the country.

At that time, Wayne had just completed his very first eating contest, which was a pizza competition. He had placed fourth, behind the first three winners who were all professional competitive eaters. Placing fourth was a revelation that he could be as good as any of them. "That's why I became interested in eating contests," he admits. As the top amateur, Wayne received $100 as a consolation prize.

The recognition he received and the fact that he could compete alongside professional competitive eaters motivated Wayne and he began looking for other contests to join. He chanced upon the balut contest in New York which also appealed to his Filipino heritage.

His mother and father never taught Wayne about balut, because as he describes it, "they themselves will not eat it." Although his dad ate it while growing up, Wayne notes his dad never did care for it and nor did his mother.

Participating in eating contests has given him the experience of making new friends and traveling to new places. "It's nice. You make friends along the way," Wayne explains. "When I first started, it was about the excitement of doing the contest. But as I go along, it's all about the experience. I go to random places I've never been before. And the people you meet. I've made some really good friends out of this." For Wayne, it is clear that via culinary capital, he also has obtained social capital which he has parlayed into a cosmopolitan lifestyle.

Wayne's other eating feats consist of different foods, not just balut. He lists the other foods he has consumed in competitive eating contests: pizzas, tacos, burgers, sausages, kimchi, burritos, macaroni and cheese, pickles, Japanese curry, chicken wings, super hot chicken wings, peppers, oysters, pie, dumplings, gelato, a type of pastry called kolachis, Jamaican beef patties, Bolivian soltenas, bagels, and more recently, Carolina Reapers.

Although he was not familiar with some of the foods, Wayne still tried them all within the confines of the eating contest. Balut was one of those foods that he tried for the first time ever while in competition. "Oh yeah, I'm always open to eating anything," Wayne says, proud of being an omnivore. "But one of the things that attracted me to these eating contests is, I love food. I think most people that do eating contests love food. That's why they joined the contest in the first place."

But the media coverage of the balut contest was "intense," as Wayne describes it. He believes it was magnified by the fact that the contest was not just about competitive eating but also an event which promoted Filipino culture. "Most contests are just standard pizza or hamburgers or hot dogs," Wayne notes. "You never hear about balut being in a contest. The fact that we're celebrating a Filipino food in general—that's like the only Filipino food contest that I know of."

The restaurant owners, the sponsors of the contests, also deliberately courted the spotlight, according to Wayne:

> The difference is the owners also played a big aspect of promoting themselves as well … most people, they have a contest, and they don't really promote it, they'd advertised it in the restaurant or what not. But the owner of the Maharlika restaurant, Nicole [Ponseca], she definitely got it because she wanted to bring more attention to Filipino culture as well as her restaurant, that's how I feel. Because most places wouldn't have a contest to attract new customers and get everyone excited. It's usually just a local thing … With

her, it's promoting Filipino culture in a very big way so I think that's one of the aspects why this one was promoted socially more.

The balut-eating contest definitely drew in the spotlight to the two restaurants, Jeepney and Maharlika, and the buzz was even noticed by Anthony Bourdain who noted in an interview on CNN that "there is a very hot hipster restaurant currently in New York where hipsters with ironic facial air and sunglasses are lined up 12 feet deep to get in and eat this" (Piers Morgan Live 2013). Wayne points to restaurant owner Nicole Ponseca as a strong business woman who uses her Filipino heritage as part of her strategy to be noticed.

The cultural approach clearly has worked: the restaurants and balut have been featured in blogs, traditional news media, and YouTube videos viewed by tens of thousands. Commoditization of the culture via balut has undeniably brought recognition to Jeepney and Maharlika. Thanks in part to balut-eating as a performance generating culinary capital, the restaurants' profile was raised and they are now arguably an integral part of the new Filipino food moment (Gold 2017).

There is no doubt in Wayne's mind that if the contest was one featuring a more traditional food, for example, *adobo*, then it would not have garnered that much attention. It is balut's primal appearance, not its taste, that has made it a celebrity. Describing balut, Wayne shares the following details. "I told everyone after the first contest, the taste was like a boiled egg with a soupy broth, that's what it tasted like to me." The fertilized egg tastes too tame for Wayne's taste buds. "It's not that I don't like it; it's something that's not on my list of things to eat. I'm a big food person. It's good but it never wows me. It has to have that wow factor."

Wayne is not the only competitive eater who feels that balut is lacking in flavor. Sergio Raya is a Mexican American competitive eating athlete who looks far younger than his 40-some years. Sergio had never eaten balut until he placed second in Pistahan's contest in 2016. I interviewed him immediately after the contest and by phone and followed up via email.

Although the contest was the first time he ate balut, Sergio had heard about it before from a Filipino friend when he was growing up. His 14-year-old brother had also eaten it, but Sergio never wanted to try. As an adult, he heard about balut again from his Filipino coworkers but was put off by its appearance.

ıring balut to garlic, which he also does not like, Sergio notes that
ıat it again if he had to do it. However, it is not a food that he would
..ormally go out and buy unless it was a special occasion like an eating contest, party, or festival.

"Nah, the only time I would eat it would be at the competition again. It's not something I would buy at the store. Maybe if I was to buy it, I would put condiments on it. Like vinegar or salt, that's always better." The balut served at the competition was bland, according to Sergio, which was fine since "you have to shove it down your throat."

A competitive eater for 10 years, Sergio loves food. For the last several years, he has averaged 10–12 eating contests a year. "I like the excitement, and the adrenalin rush. Now it's a dream come true, win or lose, it's fun."

Sergio credits the movie *Stand by Me* as the catalyst that prompted him to participate in eating competitions. His favorite scene was when the character nicknamed "Lardass" competed in a blueberry pie-eating contest. Watching the scene unfold, Sergio recalls thinking that would be "really cool" to do.

But it was only when he was 32 years old that he finally saw his first eating contest in person, a Fourth of July pie-eating competition held in Great America, in Santa Clara, California. He joined and promptly won for consuming a whole apple pie. The prize was free admission tickets to the amusement park. Sergio was hooked.

These days, when not working for the Frito-Lay Inc., a subsidiary of PepsiCo, Sergio travels from his Bay Area home to places like Sacramento, where he competes in the corn dog-eating contest at the California State Fair. It is one of the more difficult eating contests he has competed in, as it is a two-day affair. In 2015, he ate 10 corn dogs and the following year, he consumed 11 and placed sixth. The corn dog contest has five tiers of prizes, with a first prize of $2,500, second prize of $2,000, third prize of $1,500, fourth prize of $500, and fifth prize of $100.

"I like to have fun in the contest, but if I win, it's even more fun. I will do it for a trophy or a certificate," he says.

In 2016, Sergio's winnings totaled an estimated $2,500 in prizes, whether cash or gift cards. Included was a $500 certificate for a local hot springs resort. For winning the "7 mile House Cow Palace" hamburger-eating contest, he received the prize of a free Cow Palace burger for one whole year anytime he feels like stopping in at the restaurant. To appreciate his achievement, each Cow Palace hamburger is equivalent to about two big Macs and French fries. Sergio was able to eat one Cow Palace burger in 2.5 minutes.

When not competing, Sergio works out and spends time with his family. He runs 20 miles a week, lifts weights, and does martial arts every day. To prepare for competitive eating, a few days before the contest, he trains his stomach by drinking a gallon of milk along with eating normal-sized meals.

Competitive eating is definitely a sport to him:

> You have to figure out the quickest way to eat the food. There's always someone better than you. You have to figure out your opponent. Your opponent is the food. The bratwurst is different from balut, taters is different from a hot dog.

But for Sergio, eating balut is the most difficult contest of all. "The balut contest goes down as the toughest contest mentally because I had to try not to look at it and concentrate on the flavor, which tasted like boiled chicken."

If there's one thing that Sergio wants people to know about balut, it's "not as bad as it looks." According to him, people criticize balut because they have never tried it. "I'm pretty sure that if they had condiments, some kind of a hot sauce, or a little salt, it would be pretty good."

He has no doubt that balut will be known even more throughout the world:

> I think it will spread in popularity because of social media, and television shows like *Bizarre Foods* in the Travel Channel. People know what it is, because they've seen what it is. They are discouraged because of how it looks but they don't know what it tastes like.

It should be stated at this point that competitive eating is already out-of-reach for many who may be food-insecure and unable to obtain the time and means to be able to travel to compete in eating contests. Both Sergio and Wayne (and others in the competitive eating field) can be seen as a type of "foodie" in their demonstration of omnivorousness which creates their ability to generate social and cultural capital for themselves.

Defining what is economic, social, and cultural capital is required here. Pierre Bourdieu, in his key article, "The Forms of Capital," defined these three types of capital (Bourdieu [1983] 1986). Bourdieu described economic capital as that which can directly be transformed into money, social capital as having "connections" or network of social relations that can, in the right circumstance, be converted into economic capital, and cultural capital which has three forms: embodied, where one cultivates or work "at oneself" to develop skills and personality; objectified such as ownership of material goods, and institutionalized, where cultural capital is bestowed for example, by an academic institution in the form of a degree. Unlike economic capital which is visible, cultural capital is difficult to quantify so it operates more as "symbolic capital" and having it enables one to improve social standing and the ability to climb up the economic ladder (Bourdieu [1983] 1986:241–248).

As competitive eaters, it can be argued that both Wayne and Sergio already possess social and cultural capital which is being used to generate economic capital. In addition, excelling in competitive eating has also allowed them to acquire culinary capital. Whether it is their ability to eat foods in amounts that defies the norms of society or their willingness to try foods that have been stigmatized like balut, Wayne and Sergio (and other competitive eaters like them) reap recognition and status through their eating pursuits (Naccarato and LeBesco 2012). This culinary capital continues to accumulate each time they participate in yet another contest. Winning such events can enable them to eventually gain access to all three forms of capital as defined by Bourdieu ([1983] 1986). They have become culinary experts with authority who can make recommendations to other consumers who respect their opinions and suggestions (see Naccarato and LeBesco 2012:67). That culinary experts can be both chefs and esteemed food critics as well as competitive eating athletes is proof of the contradictory ways that culinary capital circulates.

As Naccarato and LeBesco caution, however, "it is clear that both models are available only to those with the economic resources and cultural capital to adopt them" (2012:10). Simply put, although it may seem that competitive eating is a sport that is open to "every man" (Naccarato and LeBesco 2012:103–104), it is not easily obtainable by others who may aspire to emulate but cannot do so due to a host of limitations that may include economic and physical reasons.

Culinary capital is no longer limited to the rich and the elite, but also to those who are able to demonstrate an omnivorousness or openness to eating experiences which results in having an extensive food knowledge. The rise in culinary tourism has also merged with the notion of omnivorousness as more people become open to experiencing other foods from various cultures. As many become comfortable with different foods, that in turn expands the boundaries of their taste buds about what is good or edible to eat (Long 2004). The presence of adventurous eaters whether due to culinary tourism or omnivorousness results in culinary capital becoming within reach for many.

## Competitive eating, stunt or eating contest?

Although balut may now grace the stage of many an eating contest, actual competitive eating has been a fixture in the United States since the late 1700s. Such unbridled occasions for gobbling may have started as reactions against the restrictive dictates which governed European ways of consumption, and the freedom to eat enormous amounts suited American notions of food abundance and individuality (Kaufman 2009; Vardi 2010).

The ways balut has been talked about and shown on television and online can reveal how Asian Americans, particularly Filipino Americans, are still considered as "savages" who eat "exotic" fare such as embryonic eggs and dog meat. As such, an analysis of balut-eating contests can benefit from a comparison with the eating contests which featured African Americans during the turn of the twentieth century in America.

Called "racial eating contests" by Itai Vardi, these events were commonly occurring spectacles of entertainment where African Americans were made to compete against each other in "gorging competitions" that served to justify the racial stereotypes which included not just their supposed physical characteristics but also their alleged differences in culinary appetites (Vardi 2010). Applying Pierre Bourdieu's notion of cultural capital and Franz Fanon's concept of the "racializing gaze," Vardi argues that such contests reinforced widely held beliefs and practices about the inferiority of African Americans. Staged mostly by whites for a white audience, these "black-based eating contests for whites' pleasure flourished in the post-Reconstruction era" (Vardi 375). Such contests could be seen as efforts by whites to create boundaries between themselves and African Americans that governed interactions according to racial lines in Jim Crow-era America (Vardi 2010:373). These contests typically took place during social events to entertain attendees and their families including a 1908 Elk luncheon meeting in Dallas, a 1916 National Fertilizer Association conference in Hot Springs, Virginia, and a cycling club meeting in New York in 1892 (Vardi 2010:377).

When balut is eaten in eating competitions without cultural context, such events may have more in common with the racial eating contests as defined by Vardi. But whereas Vardi found that individual agency was limited during these early cultural practices, balut-eating contests in the twenty-first century held largely by Filipino Americans for other Filipino Americans as well as non-Filipinos are events that can be seen as challenging the status quo. As such, I argue that when such occurrences are properly introduced with a defined cultural context for an audience of largely Filipino Americans and others who are genuinely curious with a desire to learn about the culture, then these contests can be seen as positive examples of encounters "between races that is not based on denial and fantasy" (hooks 1992:371).

A definition of competitive eating is needed here before further examination of the balut-eating contest phenomena and the possible reasons why balut has come to be a food chosen to be highlighted at such events. As noted before, there are many other Filipino dishes that have more appeal for Western palates.

Although I have been using the term "contests," scholar Lawrence Rubin defines three distinct types of eating challenges. Competitive eating is "a contest of skill, in this case eating voluminously and/or rapidly for remuneration, which may or may not be monetary" and where the stakes can also include winning fame and publicity (Rubin 2008:250). In comparison, an eating contest is "a highly localized and informal stakes-based challenge between opponents who are known to each other through family and/or community ties," while an eating stunt is "a monetary or pride-based challenge" involving items not usually eaten by people, such as the eating of small live animals in reality television shows (Rubin 2008:250).

A balut-eating contest, however, defies the neat categories of what makes an eating stunt, a contest or a competitive eating event. This is because it combines elements of all three. It is a competitive eating event because participants consume many balut in a short amount of time to garner some kind of reward, such as money and visibility. It is an eating contest because it can also be an informal event that involves opponents who may be familiar with each other within the tight Filipino American community whether in San Francisco or Maui or New Jersey. And it is an eating "stunt" in the eyes of non-Filipino audience members because the food being consumed is not typically part of what they consider to be a "normal diet." But for those of Filipino heritage, a balut-eating contest is less of a stunt because whether or not balut is part of their everyday diet in the United States, it is a part and parcel of familiar Filipino culture. What would be the stunt factor is the fact that it is unusual to eat numerous balut in such a short amount of time.

Balut featured on television features more of a stunt factor. The producers of *Fear Factor* use the format of focusing on one contestant's performance at a time to dramatize and aggregate the "multiple levels of disgust" experienced by its viewers (Halloran 2004:35). This is done by focusing on the item, watching individual contestants eat it, then viewing how they throw up and then try to "psych out" their competitors (Halloran 2004:35–36).

Whether called an eating contest or competitive eating, an occasion involving the rapid consumption of balut for a trophy, money, and visibility in the community attracts a mixture of audience and participants from different backgrounds which lead to varying expectations of the event. If one is introduced to balut through the medium of reality television, the event is likely perceived as an eating stunt, but if the culture broker consists of parents, relatives, and friends, then it is more of an eating contest that can bring the participant "15 Minutes of Fame" within the community and quite possibly beyond. That visibility may lead to culinary capital which can be further used to create agency for competitive eating champions like Wayne Algenio.

The balut-eating contest resembles the standard all-American eating contest, whether involving pies or hot dogs. As mentioned above, the New York contest was influenced by Nathan's Hot Dog-eating contest which reportedly began in 1916 and in other accounts, 1918 (Rubin 2008). Pie-eating contests are older, and although such events have now come to symbolize Americana, the first written record of a pie-eating contest took place in Toronto, Canada, in 1878 (Lohman 2016).

Balut-eating contests may be seen an offshoot of these pie-and-hot-dog-eating contests, and as such, they are familiar to many Filipino Americans and others in the United States. Yet they are a unique combination of nationalism and identity-making for a group of immigrants who are no longer afraid of being seen and heard. Taken from the back stage to the front stage, from private homes into in-your-face contests, balut contests are sites where cultural negotiation is taking place. Its appearance in heritage festivals and competitions illustrates how food can be used to mark boundaries (Kalcik 1984). Both participants and organizers as well as some audience viewers can proclaim themselves as members of the Filipino American community who are engaged in the negotiation of their cultural identities away from the motherland through competition with one another and others who are non-Filipino.

## A localized genre

By examining stereotypes involving food like watermelon and chicken, Psyche Williams-Forson (2006) explores how food has been utilized to denigrate African Americans. Analyzing racist images in advertising, film, and television and other materials, she shows how the dominant representation of African Americans portrayed them as caricatures. In the case of balut, its portrayal in the mainstream media is illustrative of the racialization that permeates social discourse, including the discourse involving food (Ku et al. 2013).

If, however, enterprising Filipino Americans choose to play up the foreign nature of balut, the encounter is a limited one that perpetuates the fantasy and the long history of the ethnic being displayed and Western audiences being agog at the display of such difference. For the most part, balut-eating contests offer the "ethnic" some agency via his or her performance and one is able to garner culinary capital off the appetites of Westerners for new and exotic foods (see Heldke 2003). Even if it is staged for the amazement of the non-Filipino audience members, these contests can still contain moments of edification and clarification. The winner of the contest also gains recognition and culinary capital, as whoever wins in a festival competition establishes a symbolic power over others (Falassi 1987:6).

In general, I submit that balut-eating competitions are staged more for the benefit of Filipino Americans who want to be finally "heard" and "seen" in their adopted homeland. It is a way to be noticed and situated among other immigrant groups, as well as participate in one of the hallmarks of American culture. After all, what is more American than an eating contest held during a fair or a festival?

For some festival-goers and contestants who are of Filipino heritage, balut is a symbolic marker of Filipino-ness, so eating it is to enforce one's pride in being a Filipino. The act of consumption may even be tinged with nostalgia, and as stated previously, homesick migrants get a chance to ingest the homeland in their bodies with each bite. In this case, balut-eating serves both to mark cultural difference and it functions as a temporary remedy while one is displaced (see Mannur 2007:13).

A half-century ago, folklorist Dan Ben-Amos decried the incongruity between what he called "ethnic genres" or local genres and those analytical categories of genres such as tales, myths, and legends that scholars constructed to examine cultural phenomena (Ben-Amos [1969] 1976:215). In short, he drew attention to the ethnic genre or native cultural expression in its context instead of privileging the classification that academics use to examine cultural phenomena. Genre (or *genus* as the term stems from Latin) refers to "'a class' or 'a kind' that allows many disparate, and often related, concepts to be conveniently divided and subdivided" (Harris-Lopez 2003:99). In folkloristics, genre refers to categories of traditions, intangible to the tangible, including beliefs, games, myths, songs, rituals, wood-carving traditions, jokes, riddles, and rhymes, as well as eating contests.

Ben-Amos urged for the "local" styles or a particular group's emic or internal genres to be recognized and his recommendation remains valid even today. Such events as balut-eating contests, where the performance of identity can be seen, cannot be classified simply to fit into a general genre of a festival game or eating contest. I suggest that instead, it can be seen as a localized genre which communicates a group's experiences and influences around them.

Ben-Amos defines ethnic genres as "a self-contained system by which society defines its experiences, creative imagination, and social commentary," which can also be further understood as "cultural metafolklore" (Ben-Amos [1969] 1976:226) as it is a particular group's commentary of its own cultural situational context. Ben-Amos's notion of the "ethnic genre" renders the native voice to be "empowered" and for the local practices to be respected (Zhang 2020:forthcoming).

With this understanding, the genre of competitive eating in Asian American heritage contests can then be seen in the context of Filipino Americans creating their own interpretation or their own localized genre that is an extension as well as a commentary on the mainstream American folklore around them, such as all-American fairs and pie-eating contests. In this respect, balut-eating contests have developed as cultural metafolklore with an eye toward indigenizing the particular genre of pie-eating contests to reflect the specificity of the Filipino American experience. This shared experience is one that reflects nostalgia, is touched by colonization and driven by the continued discrimination of their foods in Western shows, blogs, and social media, thus influencing the creation of this type of hybrid-genre where the focus is on who eats the most balut (which can be interpreted as who is the most "Filipino") within a set limit of time.

Participants, no matter their ethnicity, partake in a cultural activity that traditionally has been a litmus test of how "Filipino" one is. Such contests offer a "culinary citizenship" which has been defined as "a form of affective citizenship which grants subjects the ability to claim and inhabit certain subject positions via their relationship to food" (Mannur 2007:13). Affective citizenship is used here to mean the emotions that citizens feel about themselves, other citizens, and their nation (Zembylas 2013:6). This type of citizenship via the culinary route can incorporate traditional scripts of who is Filipino as well as other possibilities of belonging.

In the Filipino folkloric system, such challenges as eating balut have already existed in the form of daring others, either Filipinos from the diaspora who have never been "home" or have been absent for quite a while, as well as those who are foreign-born from another heritage. The Oxford Dictionary defines "dare" "to have the courage to do something, defy or challenge (someone) to do something, take the risk of; brave." I was dared by my mother to eat balut as a young child growing up in the Philippines. To "dare" someone to eat balut is a typical form of initiation into eating the food that can be seen between family members, friends, and casual acquaintances within the Philippine culture but does not draw as much attention as when a Filipino dares someone from outside of the culture to eat balut. This dare, a localized genre in the Philippines which has been remarked on (Matejowsky 2013), was further influenced by Western reality television shows such as *Fear Factor* and *Survivor*. The result of the intermingling is a transformation to another type of cultural expression, that of balut-challenge eating contests. Within this local genre as it is found in the United States, Filipino Americans can perform both their Filipino and American identities in a public setting such as a festival. In the end, balut-eating contests remain consistent with the rules of the original Filipino genre, where one is successfully integrated into the group/situation by rising to the challenge or to have the willingness to perform an act considered "Filipino" or filipinizing.

As a native genre, these eating contests have the earmarks of artistic communication, including a performance with opening and closing, which involve framing, as well as themes (see Ben-Amos 1971). Such performances which now take place in the wider arena of American festivals and celebrations, may be setting the stage for the greater integration (not necessarily full acceptance) of Filipino immigrants in American society. Whether Filipino Americans are readily subsumed into the more mainstream arena of American society in this age of building walls instead of bridges is debatable. Eating a balut egg is an act that may always raise the eyebrows (and shackles), of more than a few people.

Although Ben-Amos limits his discussion of localized expressions to the "verbal arts" or oral modes of communication, his plea for the consideration and use of the so-called ethnic genres remain useful decades later in the re-conceptualization of what makes Asian American cultural expressions, or the folklore of those schooled in the culture of both the motherland and the adopted country. Juwen Zhang has further examined such diasporic expressive culture, using the term "folkloric identity" which he defined as "*what folklore a group practices* in the making of their group identity" (Zhang 2015).

It seems that balut is a perfect food to feature in an eating contest because it successfully draws attention with its "extreme" reputation, a food with an ability to provoke a reaction more often than not in today's reality-crazed society. It is a lightning rod and a touchstone of the current sociopolitical and economic contexts experienced by Filipino Americans today. The contests are a kind of performance that uses the marker of food to construct identity as Filipinos in America via the "outing" of a once-private, insider food. That the contests are taking place in festivals is fitting as such events tend to occur in places where selected foods are carefully curated by insiders to the culture, with certain "esoteric" foods that might be found unpalatable for average mainstream consumption kept out-of-sight for insider use (Magliocco 1993).

This chapter attempts to recognize these balut-eating contests as a local genre with the ability to "empower the group to establish equal discourse at a broader scale" (Zhang 2020:forthcoming). The use of balut to reconstruct the folkloric identity of Filipino Americans is deliberate and intended for all to see. In examining these contests via the lens of folkloric identity, one is able to move away from the idea of an "ethnic" group and the notion of "authentic" folklore, as now the focus is on what a group is practicing or doing to make its group identity (Zhang 2020:forthcoming). It is also a broad enough concept to encompass other, non-Filipino groups that are also utilizing the same markers, whether it be balut or something else, in order to achieve their new identities.

From the description of the contest in a festival website and local newspapers, to the choice of music from a Filipino American artist and the decor which includes the Philippine flag on the hat of the winning participant, balut-eating contests are a way for Filipino Americans to announce and construct their identities publicly. These events are also not limited to those claiming Filipino heritage but also include those foodies who want to be distinct (Johnston and Baumann 2010) and who want to take advantage of the endless search for the exotic and the authentic (Bendix 1997; Heldke 2003).

The contests illustrate the "anti-elitism" that predominates in competitive eating and exemplifies how culinary capital can be accessed (Naccarato and Lebesco 2012:100) in the consumption of a much-maligned food. In addition to challenging mainstream perceptions of the proper diet and decorum, the contests contribute to understanding how some Filipino Americans are negotiating their identities in the age of media and technology while resisting the vilification of their cultural practices.

The fact that balut is a formerly insider food that is now "overtly displayed" to proclaim a symbolic identity for Filipino Americans reveals that the line between private consumption versus public ingestion has been removed for the most part. In this age of shock television, this once-reserved food that was consumed with such insider dishes as dinuguan (pork blood stew) is now prominently in the front and center in balut-eating festivals, communicating to the outside world that Filipino Americans are here to stay.

# Balut: The Super Clickbait of the Internet

In 2018, the "Balut Challenge" is available to anyone willing to consume it. Typing the words "balut challenge" online produces videos ranging from thousands of views to 10 million clicks of alleged first-time consumers trying this cultural delicacy. That more people are aware of this food in this era of accelerated globalization, technology, and mass media is hardly surprising. This is in contrast to the late 1990s, when I first started writing about the cultural consumption of balut, and there were only a handful of articles in newspapers and magazines and virtually no scholarly treatment of this foodway except for Doreen Fernandez's essays.[1]

The Balut Challenge is one of the many food challenges available to be viewed online. The *surströmming* challenge, which involves opening a can of the Swedish fermented fish delicacy, and the durian[2] challenge, where people try the tropical fruit with a distinct smell, come closest to the balut challenge but it is arguably the embryonic egg that is the most famous.

For this chapter, I will draw on my observations of popular culture, from television reality shows to social media blogs/vlogs. I ask why this food has gained such a worldwide audience and what might be the motivating factors behind this type of consumption. How might it differ from traditional use, who are the participants and what are their shared ways of thinking (Bronner 2009:29)?

## Reality television bites balut

Before summarizing Balut Challenge videos and noting its typology, a short description of the history and impetus for these videos is needed. I had suggested that the rise of balut's popularity can be linked directly to its appearance in the show *Fear Factor* in 2002, a possible *terminus ante quem* for balut challenge contests. Reality television mania was at a fever pitch during the early 2000s and *Fear Factor*, Season 2, Episode 13, featured contestants eating two balut eggs in three minutes to continue on to the finals. Balut later went on to star in subsequent episodes of the show.

Balut became a regular feature in other shows like *Amazing Race Australia 2* where teams had to eat eight balut eggs in order to advance, and *Hell's Kitchen* where it was fed to contestants, some of whom gagged and vomited on television. Other shows like travel-and-food series Anthony Bourdain's *No Reservations* and *Bizarre Foods with Andrew Zimmern* used balut as a way to shore up the hosts' savvy reputation of eating every food possible as a hook to lure in viewers.

Balut's publicity profile further got a boost by the fact that Filipino Manny Pacquiao, who reigned as the most famous boxer in the world for the first decade of the twenty-first century, was known to include balut in his regular diet, crediting its nutritional powers for his boxing prowess (Vick 2016), in addition to his consumption of warm milk and beef broth soup. If one was to extrapolate using the Pacman's example and the star power of balut in various television shows, it seems the conclusion drawn in the end by the average viewer is simply this: in order to win, one must consume the egg. What one is exactly "winning" will be further described below.

Although *Fear Factor* may have first introduced balut to a worldwide audience, it is perhaps *Survivor* that succeeded in cementing the word "challenge" next to the word "balut." The television series made its debut in 1997 and has since gone on to have 36 seasons as of 2018. Its main premise involves contestants who must fend for themselves in a remote location with the challenges of finding shelter and food without being eliminated for the ultimate goal of winning one million dollars. It is widely credited as the show that launched the reality television craze (Augustyn 2018). Contestants in *Survivor* must face additional "immunity challenges" which if passed, allows them to have a better chance at winning the prize.

Balut has been featured regularly as an "immunity challenge" throughout the two decades of the show. In 2004 for example, the tenth season of *Survivor* which was filmed in Palau involved castaways who had to eat five balut within a short period of time. That season gained *Survivor* an Emmy Award nomination. In the 26th season, the show debuted *Survivor: Caramoan—Fans vs. Favorites* which aired in 2013 and was filmed in the secluded Caramoan Islands in the Philippines. Balut was featured as the first of the individual immunity challenges that contestants had to face.

The setting of Caramoan, which has subsequently starred in later international editions of *Survivor*, is a character in its own right. When interspersed with the seemingly primeval and "simple" balut, which host Jeff Probst introduces in the beginning of the show as originating from the Philippines, the location itself becomes magnified in the viewer imagination as this wild place where one is left to eat whatever nature can provide. The geographic specificity of the place and linking of balut to the location increases the authenticity factor of balut. Locating balut to this place amplifies the experience of the "sauvage" and by its association to wilderness, intensifies the Otherness of this food which has been clearly tied to an "ethnic" group of people.

Balut's appearance in this 26th season of *Survivor* also offers viewers a chance to reminisce about the previous appearances of balut in the show, aiding in the formation of a tradition where the food is associated with disgust. Describing his experience in Caramoan, contestant Matthew Freburg shared that "competing in a food eating challenge on *Survivor* is pretty cool for a fan of the show. It's one of the original challenges, and participating makes you feel connected—if only via disgust—to old school legends" (Ross 2017) (Figure 23). Freburg added that balut "tastes as disgusting as it looks," but it was consuming pig's brains that was the most punishing long after the fact (Ross 2017).

But to veteran host Jeff Probst, there is no question that balut is the most "disgusting" dish ever to be offered as a food challenge. "Those little heads, that tiny body, those light feathers," was how Probst first described balut in an interview with *Entertainment Weekly* to publicize the new season of *Survivor*. He stated that "the craziest part of all, those are sold in Asian supermarkets in the same manner we sell potato chips" (Ross 2018).

The appeal of balut, or rather, the emphasis on the "repellant" nature of balut which draws in the viewer, can be seen in an image of a broken embryonic egg surrounded by its liquid on a wooden platter in *Survivor*'s Twitter feed (Figure 24). Posing the question "Would you eat this to win?" further encapsulates in the viewer's mind that to overcome this food challenge would somehow bring some kind of prize. The picture, much like the homemade and

**Figure 23** Photo Still from *Survivor: Caramoan*—Courtesy of Survivor Productions, LLC.

**SURVIVOR** ✓
@survivorcbs

Follow ⌄

Oh, just some balut for the final round of this
#ImmunityChallenge. Would you eat this for
the win? #Survivor

Retweets   Likes
49         141

5:38 PM - 28 Oct 2015

79      49      141

**Figure 24** Photo Still from *Survivor: Caramoan*—Courtesy of Survivor Productions, LLC.

professional videos of balut, is designed to provoke some kind of reaction, most likely one of fascinated aversion, from the viewer. The veins crisscrossing the yolk and the albumen in the Twitter picture while sitting on a puddle of liquid is clickbait extraordinaire.

By 2013, when *Survivor: Caramoan—Fans vs. Favorites* production debuted, viewers in the Western world had formed its opinion of the food. If imitation is the best form of flattery, the appearances of these myriad videos of Balut Challenge that were spawned after the show can be seen as a sort of tribute to the success of the reality program. These videos feature wannabe *Survivor* contestants in their own immunity challenge. To "survive" the feat of consuming the egg can entail more than acquiring bragging rights. One can also pretend to live like reality television heroes and heroines by garnering economic, social, and cultural capital via the number of clicks which bring on the "gazes" of multiple viewers who can be turned to regular, monetized subscribers.

## Balut challenge videos: Staging identities

These days, as anyone with a computer can see, searching the words "balut" and "balut challenge" will pull up numerous videos of people from all over the world eating balut. Curiously, many videos feature individuals who are non-Filipinos. A sample of the titles include "Australians Try Balut," "Spanish People Try Balut," "American Tries Balut" (there are quite a number of these variations with the word "American" in it), "Mexicans Eat Balut," "White People Eating Balut for the First Time" (which again is a popular title with several variations), and "Foreigners Try Balut."

From the titles, the point of these videos is obvious. It is all about the first time one encounters the partially developed duck, with the focus on the image and performance of the "plucky" eater. There is usually no attempt to simulate the social conditions where one typically eats the egg, and no cultural context is provided which could instruct or teach viewers how to properly eat the egg. The majority of these Balut Challenge videos emphasize, instead, the novice eater gearing up resolve to "conquer" the challenge and the chronicling of the "hardships" involved in eating this food.

In the majority of these short films, the consumers refer to seeing the challenge in videos or reality television shows. Based on the format, the spoken words or "script," and the inevitable food challenge in the form of eating balut, it becomes clear that the people in the videos were influenced by, and exposed to, the consumption of balut through the conduit of the media, both mainstream and social. This is but one example how "electronic media provide resources for self-imagining as an everyday social project" (Appadurai 1996:4).

This explosion of material in the form of blogs/vlogs and videos has been watched by millions of viewers, as evidenced by the number of clicks. Sometimes, the Filipino cultural belief that balut is an aphrodisiac and a natural Viagra for men is explained at the outset of the video; most of the time, it is not. These short films all share the following in common: the viewer is invited to participate as the performer eats balut for the first time or an experienced individual teaches a newbie how to eat it, with many shots panning to the newbie's face as well as the fertilized egg which has been torn apart for all the world to see.

A rough typology of Balut Challenge videos can be gleaned from the titles and content. The most popular seems to fit under the theme of "White person (usually an American) Tries Balut for the First Time." This category contains the subgenre of "Foreigner Tries Balut" and also the subgenre of "Well-known Actor/Personality Tries Balut."

Examples of this subgenre of celebrities taking up the challenge to eat balut include one starring actor Zac Efron who tried it on his first visit to the Philippines in 2012. He subsequently charmed Filipinos even more when he declared it delicious. Then there is the video of magician David Blaine being tutored by champion world boxer Manny Pacquiao on how to eat balut and durian, which has been viewed over 386,000 times as of February 23, 2019. Reactions to the videos are usually supportive of the fact that the celebrities tried a Filipino snack food.

Another major category may also be understood as having the theme of "Filipino Tries Balut to Show Others." The video usually consists of Filipinos or Filipino Americans teaching others from different ethnicities (although the Filipino protagonist usually notes that he has not had balut since he was a young child). The majority of the time, this type of production features male performers. These videos that star Filipinos as the main character or side character teaching Westerners are usually not as popular as videos of Westerners trying the egg.

The exception to this seem to be those Balut Challenge shows featuring YouTube personality Guava Juice (a.k.a. Roy Fabito), who is a Filipino American. He has at least two videos featuring balut, including "Egg vs. Fertilized Duck Egg! (Balut Challenge!)" that was released on YouTube on May 9, 2017, and "Eating Duck Embryos (Balut) Philippines Trip Part Final" that was first shown on April 7, 2015. The two videos have been viewed over two million times. Interestingly, the latter video which shows Guava Juice on his trip to the Philippines has received less clicks despite being available since 2015. As of February 23, 2019, it had only been seen 651,000 times as opposed to the one released in 2017 which had over 1.4 million. Could it be that viewers preferred the sensationalized version without the cultural context?

Besides the titles evoked above, Balut Challenge videos are also advertised with various titles such as "Japanese Eating Balut," "Non Filipino Eating 'Balut' for the First Time," "Swiss Guy Tries Balut," "!BALUT! First Indian Tries Balut!!!," and "Korean Tries Balut." All these would fall under the theme of "Foreigner Tries Balut." The majority of the Balut Challenge videos, however, are clearly influenced by reality television productions. A small portion of those starring Filipinos or who have Filipino performers may also be drawing from the long-standing tradition in the Philippines of encouraging other Filipinos or egging them on to try balut for the first time or the hundredth time after being away from the homeland.

Although footage of balut-eating contests in festivals are also available online, the Balut Challenge videos are mostly less concerned with the performative aspect of becoming a "Filipino" and more focused on the "bold" and "courageous" ingestion of the fertilized egg. Some of these videos even begin with a warning to viewers that the material might be found offensive. The stunt aspect of competitive eating prevails in the Balut Challenge videos where the featured consumers take on a food that is not typically part of the Western diet (Rubin 2008:250).

The eating of fertilized eggs in online Balut Challenge videos shares the same element as the eating of balut in festival contests, with both events involving the consumption of the fertilized egg. There is also the aspect of an audience being present to watch the wolfing down of balut. The audience or viewers are there to watch the spectacle of someone eating an embryonic egg or they are drawn to witness the competitive aspect of eating.

"Balut Challenge" videos, however, differ remarkably from the festival events. For one, there is less emphasis on the number of balut or the speed of consumption, but rather, the focus is on the "gross" aspect of the food. It is the performance of the consuming act, replete with grimaces, sounds, and gestures that is continually dramatized and broadcasted to the tune of millions of clicks.

The act of going to a website or listening to something online is itself performative (Bronner 2009:32). Noting that food and performance meet at several junctures, Barbara Kirshenblatt-Gimblett remarks that "*to perform is to show* ... when participants are invited to exercise discernment, evaluation, and appreciation, food events move towards the theatrical and, more specifically, towards the spectacular" (1999:2). Almost all of the Balut Challenge videos I watched were intended to be performed as entertainment, with little if any edification about the cultural item. The balut in the videos were certainly not eaten for nutritional purposes, but instead, were ingested to emphasize the eater's capability to be an omnivore or as a foodie who could defeat others too scared to eat it.

Balut Challenge videos illustrate the prevalence of the omnivorousness in the culinary world, utilized by many, including the video performers, to leverage themselves as "foodies." The star power of omnivores like the late Anthony Bourdain could be seen in the elevation of sisig, a snack item meant for drinking sessions, much like balut. Since Bourdain's declaration of sisig as his favorite Filipino dish, it has made this simple bar dish made with pig jowls omnipresent in many hip restaurants in the Philippines as well as in some upscale Filipino American restaurants. Despite the presence of many who desire to be an omnivore in the challenge videos, there are also a group of people who try balut but do not attempt to like it. Despite that fact, however, they are still able to stand "out" from the crowd.

A likely motive behind Balut Challenge videos may be that the performer is seeking to validate an identity as a foodie or champion eater through consumption of a food that has a strong "it" factor. Despite or (because of) its reputation, balut is arguably a food that can bestow a mark of distinction for the successful eater. It is a food that can be seen as "authenticating" whoever is consuming it. Discussing the tension between the idea of gastronomic authenticity versus foods that are seen as Americanized or apocryphal, Robert Ji-Song Ku writes that "authenticity is the White Whale of modern epicurism, tirelessly pursued by hungry Ahabs (e.g. cosmopolitan foodies and displaced migrants) in search of the perfect 'native' meal" (Ku 2013:37).

What else is balut but the White Whale that is arguably the "perfect" native meal? As pointed out before, its main attraction is the fact that its unadorned appearance is its "authenticating" power. The fact that it has a reputation as a food that is considered "dubious" (Ku 2013) and can be seen as "dangerous" and "polluting" (Douglas 1966) practically ensures that consumers can authenticate themselves by standing out from the crowd as an adventurer, a conqueror able to overcome what is perceived as a taboo act by many.

In filming oneself and others in the act of ingestion, the action becomes a performance akin to taking part in a stunt, meant as a practice of distinction (Bourdieu [1979] 1984) and one designed to bring in the maximum profit via the attainment of culinary capital. Such an achievement would allow those in the videos to garner admiration from one's cohort and earn status for "mastering" this food.

Discussing the dynamics of the American gastronomic field, Johnston and Baumann state that those who have the most prestige or symbolic capital are those who gravitate to "shocking or norm-breaking food" which can include things like offal as well as balut (2010:124). For culinary experts to continue to have "cultural legitimacy," it is a must to value those foods that are considered beyond the norm (Johnston and Baumann 2010:124). "Just as symbolist poetry is more esoteric and difficult than romance novels within the literary field, within the gourmet field eating offal is more esoteric and difficult" (Johnston and Baumann 124). Therefore, those who master eating offal or foods like balut are seen as a culinary "expert" who has succeeded in eating what has been stereotyped to be a sordid, nauseating item. Is it any wonder then that reward comes in the form of culinary capital for those starring in such food challenges as the Balut Challenge?

This notion of "authentic," foreign experiences propagated in travel shows and challenge videos is promised to those watching in living rooms and on computers everywhere, and a cheap way to achieve the dream is to reenact what the high priests and priestesses are consuming, an example of culinary tourism (Long 2004). In addition, because the place and the food have become intertwined, the videos can be categorized as falling on the list of activities defined as Orientalism (Ku 2013:12–13; Said 1978). Each bite of balut can be interpreted as the East being consumed by the West, and Asia's mysteries are finally revealed in part by the unveiling of the fetal egg, for all the world to see. In consuming the egg, one may be seen as symbolically devouring "the Other" in an act of domination through consumption (hooks 1992:378).

Although televised food challenges has been described as containing a feeling of community as food is "an equalizer among strangers" (Halloran 2004:40), I would say that a sense of *communitas* tends to be not evident in most of the Balut Challenge videos. This is unlike balut contests in the festivals, where the feeling of community is more palpable especially when the ultimate champion who wins is of Filipino heritage and the crowd who are mostly Filipino Americans go wild with the win.

Rather, the videos emphasize cultural difference and are designed to leave an impression of a nauseating experience that serves to disturb and alienate viewers. The estrangement from others may well be the prevailing motivation, because in separating themselves from the crowd, the performers mark themselves as different and "distinct" from the average person viewing the video. This differentiation is what buys the eating performer the status as a real foodie and helps reap the benefits of culinary capital which can consist of a higher status and power.

Many of the Balut Challenge videos from the first two decades of the twenty-first century, however, feature a cast that is distinctly of non-Filipino heritage. Widely seen and distributed, these performances usually lack cultural context to explain the background and proper way of eating one. Although the videos share some elements as the traditional test of consumption, they are clearly a specific kind of expressive culture that has emerged from the convergence of reality television with social media and technology, along with the globalization and migration of Southeast Asians which allow for would-be consumers to access embryonic eggs in the United States and other places.

Typing the words "balut challenge" in the search box at the YouTube.com site reveals the following, as of February 23, 2019:

The first 10 results are videos that have been viewed anywhere from over 39,000 times to 10 million. Nine of the 10 videos featured the duck egg chick curled up or unfurled in all its embryonic state. The titles on the videos ranged from "Mexicans eat balut" with over 42,000 views to "OMG! RARE BALUT (Aborted Duck Egg) CHALLENGE" with over 79,000 views to "Americans try Balut (Duck Embryo)" with three million views. But it was the Blind Bird Taste Challenge from *Good Mythical Morning*, a daily talk show on the YouTube channel that generated the most views at 10 million. The show features two comedians, Rhett and Link, who are among the most influential online celebrities. In this episode, the two men don blindfolds and identify the type of bird that is being fed to them. Needless to say, both of them end up spitting the balut parts that were fed to them. Their horrified and disgusted reactions are the climax of the episode.

I was admittedly surprised at the sheer number of people who watch these videos. Comparing the videos to the traditional balut challenge which functioned like an impromptu rite of initiation incorporating visitors and long-time returnees back into the cultural landscape, the videos still had that element of the "dare" but little if any other attempt to respect the cultural practice. Also different is the emphasis on the disgusted reactions of the consumer to the embryonic egg. It is what I call "the performance of disgust" that seems to be at the center stage, when in traditional balut challenges, the individual who was reluctant to consume balut usually would be shamed for not being able to go through with the act. One would almost always be apologetic, if he or she could not eat the egg.

## A canon of disgust

In the majority of the Balut Challenge videos, there is no shamefacedness. Nor is there any apology for vomiting the food. Rather, the sickened reaction is what is expected by both the audience and also the performer. With a mostly absent cultural context, vulgarity and crassness are typically demonstrated. The more the partially developed egg is illustrated in its unsheathed glory, the better for shock value. Once the performer is confronted with the egg and reacts in revulsion, the performance continues to prolong the moments of disgust.

This performance of disgust, as articulated by past reality television productions, online videos, and mainstream publications that have painted a sensationalized picture of this food as "bizarre," "weird," and "awful," makes up what I call a "canon of disgust" that owes its conceptualizing to the historical tradition of portraying foods of the Other in an exoticized light. This canon of disgust is continually fed by the monetized online productions and ironically, by even the eating contests in festivals which uses the "curiosity factor" to attract people to watch the contest. The end result, however, of the balut-eating contests in festivals is not pure capitalism but a more nuanced introduction to Filipino culture.

The canon of disgust is assisted by the fact that balut challenge productions often consist of expressions and gestures that can be recognized by everyone. When one is disgusted, there is a "gape response" or a "ritualized vomit gesture" that is seen in all humans from babies to adults and some animal species (Ku 2013:145). If the person showing disgust is near others, those individuals are often infected with the same reactions. This can be seen in the reactions of contestants on reality shows or in the numerous video-centered blogs.

When an announcer is present in these Balut Challenge videos, the contestants are dared to eat balut. Popular reasons include to "take up the challenge," to demonstrate "mind over matter," or to eat it as a reply to viewers' request as in the case of popular vloggers so that they can describe it to their audience. An additional motivation is to draw publicity to the site by the shock value of people eating something seen as dreadful by the average Westerner. Although balut is nutritious and has been described by some as having a pleasant taste of duck and rich broth, the viral videos highlight its appearance as a way to raise the fear factor. Such a negative introduction of balut further enhances what seems to be a form of punishment that the eater must undergo in the rite of initiation on the way to being considered an omnivorous foodie (Johnston and Baumann 2010). The "punishing" act is the performance that is the centerpiece of the video.

Food can be manipulated as a form of punishment, as in the case of withholding of food or when it is made "intentionally disgusting" so that eating it is a chastisement as experienced by some prisoners eating prison food (Jones 2017). The way balut is proffered on the viral videos is to play up its reputation "as a torture of an item, a bizarrely conceived if not abjectly demonic dish"

(Kilham 2011). Because it is presented in such a manner, to eat it, then, is to be "punished." Based on the popularity of the challenge videos and the posted comments, many members of the audience seemed to be enticed to watch the "suffering" of others.

Undoubtedly, there are a number of people viewing who are curious about balut and curious about strangers eating foreign things and their reactions. Although there may be different motivations for the balut-eater to take up the challenge, the audience is ultimately there to judge the effectiveness of the performance measured by the intensity of the expressive act (Bauman 1974:293). "Performance … calls forth special attention to and heightened awareness of the act of expression, and gives license to the audience to regard the act of expression and the performer with special intensity" (Bauman 1974:293).

By its mere presence, food, in this case, balut, is performative (Kirshenblatt-Gimblett 1999:1). Having balut present allows a performance to emerge whether one is establishing a Filipino identity, or performing to illustrate oneself as an omnivorous foodie, or acting as a competitive eater. The "disgusting" aspect of balut is relevant because it allows the separation of the initiate or the would-be eater from the rest of the crowd by his or her willingness to consume a food that is considered controversial by many. The would-be eater is set up in a liminal phase as he or she ponders on whether to eat it or not, and once the balut is eaten, the successful eater is incorporated back into society with his/ her new status as a "foodie" or champion eater. A rite-of-passage has been undergone with the help of the fertilized egg (see Van Gennep 1909).

The beginning of the videos from the presentation and serving of the food to the performer is already charged with anticipatory disgust. Balut is, after all, "a substance with a strong presence" (Kirshenblatt-Gimblett 1999:16), and the astonishing value of what is inside the unassuming white shell is part of the theatrics. As mentioned before, there is a traditional way of consuming the fertilized egg, which is to sip the juice from the top of the freshly boiled egg and then peel the egg before downing it in one or two bites.

However, the behavior in almost all the Balut Challenge videos is to prolong the consumption so that the egg is torn apart, bit by bit. The liquid is usually discarded, ignored, unappreciated, when that component is one of the pleasures of eating warm balut, because it tastes like comforting chicken soup. For those who have tried Chinese soup dumplings or *xiao long bao*, I would argue that balut is a naturally occurring version where one carefully pokes the top to drink the hot soup before eating the meat immediately after the liquid.

This pleasurable sensory experience, where one can taste "soup" that has been described by some Filipino Americans like "concentrated chicken broth" is lost, however, in these videos, where the balut eggs are shown already cracked without their shells and most likely cold, as those eggs in the video called "THE BALUT CHALLENGE (Featuring L.A. BEAST) Part 2" that was published online on September 26, 2013, or other videos where the egg's solid parts are the main attraction. In these videos where eating the food is clearly a performance, not for addressing hunger nor whetting the appetite, the food has been severed from being used as nourishment.

Pointing out the drastic effects that result when "when food is dissociated from eating and eating from nourishment," Barbara Kirshenblatt-Gimblett notes "such dissociations produce eating disorders, religious experiences, culinary feats, sensory epiphanies, and art" (1999:2). In the case of Balut Challenge videos, the performances are designed to be "culinary feats." This is because these videos are generally not filmed in order to show the consumption of balut as a nourishing, traditional snack, but rather as a gristly horror-filled vignette that emphasizes its visual (non) appeal. The person who consumes it succeeds in overcoming sensory obstacles to perform a culinary achievement (in the eyes of admiring viewers, who would not dare do the same).

Describing performance as a "mode of spoken verbal communication" where the performer is responsible to the audience in the successful display of "communicative competence," Richard Bauman writes that the ability to act and speak in what is considered appropriate to the situation is a competent performance (1974:293). Although Bauman was not discussing online expressive culture but rather face-to-face communication, his insights can also be applied to the performances in these challenge videos.

In these challenge films, a competent performance is one that has been viewed multiple times or goes "viral" where the performer acts in the expected manner of one who is confronted with a "formidable" challenge. The performer draws from the language and gestures used in the canon of disgust which includes theatrics as gleaned from the television shows and other similar, online productions. One is judged proficient when he or she is able to express the "revolting" experience he or she is having.

Through the sharing of the video and reactions as evidenced in the comments, the audience can evaluate if the performer was effectively able to act the familiar display of disgust complete with the "gaped" mouth and facial contortions that dissolve in the inevitable hurling or near-heaving. If the eater or performer in the Balut Challenge videos is judged competent with intensity of expression (Bauman 1974), then culinary capital is bestowed along with economic capital (Naccarato and LeBesco 2012:2). The number of clicks or the number of "likes" is a direct commentary of the success of the performance.

Much like the reactions of viewers to shows like *Fear Factor* and *Survivor*, those watching Balut Challenge videos may be experiencing *"jouissance"* or what is defined as "sensual revulsion and pleasure" several times over, first from watching the video performer react to the embryonic chick, second from the attempts to ingest the egg, and then from the inevitable post-reaction of vomiting or reacting in disgust (Halloran 2004:30–37). In describing the thrill and delight exhibited by the audience watching *Fear Factor*, Halloran compares it to the voyeurism of those "who witness executions or attend bullfights" (2004:37).

Besides stimulating viewers who are in search of prurient delights, what else can be said about such performances? It is undeniably a performance that is occurring in these numerous videos on the internet. What could be the end goal of the performer? And what is the reason why balut is being used as the highlight of these social media videos?

Based on what I have viewed, it seems that many Balut Challenge videos are made by people who are also garnering culinary capital within the subgroup of foodies who do not want to accumulate that cultural sophistication advocated by the culinary elite. This illustrates Naccarato and LeBesco's point that "culinary capital is not owned by any one segment of society but, rather, that it is continually up for grabs" (2012:111). Yes, they can taste it and show off their capabilities of acquiring the "coveted" food, but they have no reason to pretend to like the food as others in the food culinary world or those who are politically correct are inclined to do. They can express their disgust and still be able to access culinary capital with their brutal assessment and display of detestation.

The question becomes not "why balut?" but rather, "why not balut?" It is perfectly poised to provide instant "foodie" status and is associated with notions of authenticity and exoticism, which remain influential critical elements in the American food landscape (Johnston and Baumann 2010). It may not be the *Survivor* award of one million dollars, but a carefully built up system of clicks that reap the performer a certain amount of economic and social capital via the demonstration of culinary "bravery."

## Clicking to see balut

The foodie discourse in the West must necessarily include YouTube videos. In a quick summary of how profit can be made on YouTube, financial gain can come from advertisers featured in one's channel. Channels or sites that attract viewers or who generate traffic are the ones that are targeted by advertisers. In general, videos with people of non-Filipino heritage eating balut seem to be more popular and viewed more than videos of Filipinos eating balut.

The videos with non-Filipino performers tend to exhibit performances laced with more disgust and enhanced with shocking balut imagery and are likely to have more clicks than videos featuring Filipinos doing more or less the same thing. There are a few exceptions to this but from examining numerous challenge videos, more views were earned by those of non-Filipino backgrounds.

For example, on April 1, 2017, I viewed the video "Spanish People Try Balut," created two days before. It had 8,570 views. A year later, on May 22, 2018, the same video had generated close to 106,000 views.

The video "Canadian Girl Enjoys a Balut in Cagayan de Oro," which was uploaded on March 26, 2017, had generated 79,499 views as of April 1, 2017. Thirteen months later, on May 22, 2018, the same piece registered close to 535,000 views.

In comparison, "Filipinos Eating Balut for the First Time," generated 68,076 views in four months as of April 1, 2017, an amount far surpassed by the Canadian girl video in that week. More than a year later, on May 22, 2018, the same video reached close to 82,000 viewers.

Then there was a how-to tutorial on "How to eat balut as told by a 3 year old Filipino American from NJ." Uploaded in 2015, it had as of April 1, 2016, generated a mere 8,995 views. More than a year later, that number had reached almost 31,000 views. In contrast, the video "Half Australian kid eat balut" uploaded November 10, 2017 had already garnered 32,456 views in six months.

There are a number of factors that can affect the amount of traffic. Some videos feature YouTube performers known to a greater number of followers who are subscribers. Another factor is that the video may well be sponsored by companies with money to market and bring in the traffic.

I suggest the more times a Balut Challenge video is viewed, the greater chances are that the vignette was filmed as a way to make money. Without the cultural context, and with titillation as the guide, the creator/producer of such videos stands to make a profit on the number of people who are lured to the website. In addition, the challenge videos also lay bare the cyclical nature of fashion, whether in clothes or food.

Pointing out that "predilections for excess and personal pleasure" have been paired with capital before as in the case of Roman emperor Caligula's dissipations during 1 CE, Naccarato and LeBesco argue that although foodies who competitively eat and who promote unapologetic consumption of "junk" foods considered "junk" manage to accumulate culinary capital using their own criteria, they also highlight the "very arbitrariness of *which* eating practices earn privilege and bring culinary capital" (2012:111–112).

But the authors caution against a simplistic binary pitting the health-conscious elitist food discourse with the celebration of excess and elevation of "unhealthy" foods as can be seen in competitive eating events. Instead, a hybridization of foodways which mixes "high" and "low" eating is becoming more apparent. This mixed stance is one that offers the promise of sustainability and healthful eating, along with a less biased attitude toward foods that have long been labelled as "fast food" and "bad" for the body (Naccarato and LeBesco 2012:115–119).

This hybridization of food which blurs the line between healthy foods and those labeled the opposite is illustrated in balut. A former street food in Vietnam and the Philippines known for both its nutritional content and its cholesterol effect, balut has now become elevated in the temples of good eating such as Maharlika in New York. The lines drawn between haute cuisine and the food of the masses have been made imprecise in the example of balut's consumption in the Filipino diaspora.

## Amassing culinary capital

In explaining how folklore thrives in the digital and virtual world of the internet, Simon Bronner argues that the "open realm" or folk realm of the web is a space where individuals can be participants in tradition-making (2009:22). One must re-think the old-fashioned notion of tradition as what happens out in the fields or the woods and look to how "the Internet *facilitates, mediates, or produces* tradition on a computer screen" (Bronner 2009:24). Bronner maintains that the internet is a place where creativity and "instantaneous" response is possible, and where interaction results in the fostering of "agonistic, rather than harmonious, relationships" (2009:34).

It is this "agonistic" relationship that is being encouraged in many of these Balut Challenge videos/vlogs. From the time the viewer lays eyes on the first image, which assaults the eyes, to the performance where the actor/entertainer is pitted against the subject of his/her agony, to the focus on the fetal duck in various stages of severance, each second is meant to prompt a reaction from the audience. Gratuitous shots of the balut egg from all angles aim to multiply the non visual appeal of the food and are followed up with visual shots of the expressions of inevitable fear and apprehension when faced with the embryonic duck. After conquering one's fears, the balut is eaten but there is usually a retching factor involved.

I took a closer look at several of the producers of the videos, to see who is being authenticated in these videos and why would they need to do so. One of them is Filipino American male Roi Fabito, aka as "Guava Juice" or Roy Wassabi, a 27-year-old YouTube entertainer at the time of this work, who counts more than 10 million subscribers and whose videos have been viewed more than 4 billion times. He uploads two videos a day, and as mentioned above, his segment on balut called "Egg vs. Fertilized Duck Egg! (Balut Challenge!)" where he claims to eat balut the first time has now been viewed 1.4 million times. Although of Filipino heritage, he does not provide any cultural context, nor does he follow the traditional consumption. Instead, he performs with high drama.

For example, when Roi first sees the embryo, he screams, makes faces and at one point, dangles the partially developed duck out of the shell, head first and neck exposed. Finally, he tries the balut and promptly throws up. Roi also calls on his friend, an African American, to try balut but the friend predictably regurgitates the food and walks away, leaving it unfinished. Judging from the number of views which are most likely stemming from his subscribers, Roi's balut vlog is a successful performance of disgust.

According to a nailbuzz.com article on his net worth, Roi's channel "generate an estimated revenue of around $9,000 per day ($3.3 million per year) from advertisements that run on the videos" (Julian 2018). Besides profiting from the number of views, Roi also receives income from merchandise that is available on the site. In addition to the balut challenge, Roi has been featured dunking in a bathtub full of slime and drinking his own urine. Having faced a challenge like balut-eating is another notch on Roi's belt as he is constantly on the search for extreme challenges to film. By employing the vocabulary, gestures, and facial expressions of revulsion, and most notably, an ingratiating high-pitched yell signaling his loathing, Roi Fabito actively "keeps up" with the YouTube algorithm of relevance which determines the videos the audience will be watching (Mazereeuw 2017). One can say that in Fabito's balut video, it is the lure of economic capital via culinary means which drives his performance.

Another notable example of a Balut Challenge video is perhaps that of Canadian YouTube star "Furious Pete," a 33-year-old male as of February 2019, who is known for his motivational fitness videos and competitive eating. With 4.6 million subscribers, Furious Pete filmed his first time eating balut and published his vlog on March 10, 2016. As of May, 2018, there have been close to 1.5 million views. The question "can we get this video to 10,000 likes?" is at the bottom of the screen, and Furious Pete has already more than doubled that to 24 thousand "likes." It is safe to say that Furious Pete knows what makes money and brings recognition.

Although not as big as Guava Juice or Furious Pete, KillerArt published the video "White People eating balut for the first time" on May 30, 2015. Since then, the video has been viewed 338,893 views as of February 21, 2019. KillerArt has 766 subscribers and his videos have been seen a total of 857,043 views. The balut video brought KillerArt a third of his total views.

Clicking on the link to find out who is KillerArt, I was taken to another website featuring artistic projects. It turns out that KillerArt is Jason LaJudice, a 30-something American sculptor in Texas who can be hired to create artwork; hence the appropriateness of his name. The video of balut is just a sideline meant to bring in the traffic to his real livelihood of producing sculptures for various clients.

Another example of the use of balut to "authenticate" the performer/ producer can be seen in the video titled "Balut Challenge: Aussie Team tries balut for the first time!" When I followed the link, it led me to an accounting website, called The Outsourced Accountant. Out of all the balut challenges I saw, it was one of the most thorough in providing a cultural context to the viewer. A full description of the food and how it is comparable to vegemite in Australia along with instructions on how to eat it are displayed prominently in the website below the video. Uploaded in January of 2018, the video has only been viewed several thousand times. From the respectful manner of introduction, I surmised that the video was not produced to solicit the "yuck" reaction. This was confirmed as I further investigated the company.

The Outsourced Accountant is an Australian company with offices in the Philippines employing over 700 personnel available to be hired out for accounting needs. Rather than attracting a ton of traffic from the general public, The Outsourced Accountant seems to be interested in gaining a select audience of both Philippine and Australian customers. Its use of the balut challenge in this case reveals how the Australian company is savvy enough to appeal to future business clients by illustrating how they understand the nuances of Philippine culture. By having the top managers of the firm try the fertilized egg in a respectful manner without resorting to the tired repertoire of disgust, the message is sent that they are there to appreciate the culture as well and not just to profit wholeheartedly from it.

It can be argued that The Outsource Accountant balut video exhibits a form of cultural cosmopolitanism where a Eurocentric viewpoint is avoided (see Johnston and Baumann 2010). Although most videos of the Balut Challenge tend to fall in the category of cultural food colonialism (Heldke 2003), to a lesser extent, a handful of the challenge videos may also reveal cultural cosmopolitanism or what can be defined as a desire to move away from "Eurocentrism" (Johnston and Baumann 2010:104) toward an understanding of more diverse cultural contexts. The Outsource Accountant video can be said to fall under cultural cosmopolitanism.

Cosmpolitanism originated from the Greek words for "world" and "citizen," "kosmo-polites." But instead of the common translation of "citizen of the world," the meaning is meant to be broader, with "kosmos" to mean the universe (Appiah 2019). To put it simply, cosmopolitanism refers to an expansive understanding of "other cultures and customs and a belief in universal humanity" (Anderson 1998:267). This is relevant to describe the consumption practices of those who genuinely desire to learn about others through their experience of diverse foodways. It can be seen as the opposite of cultural food colonialism (Heldke 2003).

Two of the four managers in the video expressed that it was not as bad as they thought, and even the other two who did not like it were less hostile in their description. At the end of the video, the sentence "We value culture and camaraderie, coz that's how we ROCK!" is displayed at the bottom of the screen.

Despite what may be seen as a genuine attempt to exhibit cultural cosmopolitanism, however, The Outsourced Accountant video is not above the use of balut as a profitable "clickbait." By using the balut challenge format, the company can be seen as doing their best to situate themselves as part of the foodie discourse where balut has become a prominent way to manipulate interest in the "weirdness" of the food as a way to amass culinary capital.

## Balut Challenge: A new genre of folklore on the internet

In writing about folklore in the internet, Trevor Blank states that "new traditions are being forged in online communities" (Blank 2009:18). Blank acknowledges that while there are key differences between the traditional field where folklorists have grown accustomed to studying and that of the internet, there are still similar themes in that "both have folk groups, customs, lingo and dialects, neighborhoods, crimes, relationships, commerce and various other forms of communication and education" (Blank 2009:11).

I propose that Balut Challenge videos can be seen as a new genre of expressive culture in that it exemplifies the themes that Blank describes. The videos illustrate how a local product, balut, can be marketed throughout the world for diverse consumers and could be held up as an example of glocalization (see Matejowsky 2007). Identifying this new genre can reveal the spread of cultural practices beyond traditional settings which can be appropriated and manipulated by those technologically competent to profit in today's globalized economic processes.

Rather than being a localized genre such as the balut-eating contests which I discussed in the previous chapter, the Balut Challenge video is also a new tradition with its own community composed of people who have faced the dare and have negotiated their sense of belonging, whether successful in the ingestion of the embryonic duck or not. The internet is the field, the challenge videos is the expressive culture, mirroring the traditional arena where face-to-face interaction would sometimes produce artistic communication during specific contexts.

Granted, there is no face-to-face[3] communication online but nevertheless, there is a collaborative component with the audience who leave comments on the performance. The group has its own rite of initiation eating the balut egg, and they are bound by the customary display of loathing during their performances. Their "lingo" or language of abhorrence tends to be composed of a common script with words such as "disgusting," "sick," "horrible" and any other synonym which expresses the same sentiment along those lines. With the internet acting as a camouflage for their real persona, they are able to portray their undisguised feelings which at times contain heavily racialized descriptions of a food that is beloved in Southeast Asia.

The videos are the products of their artistic endeavors to express their online identities, which lean toward the image of the food adventurer or *Survivor* contestant who is successful at overcoming the "immunity" challenge being offered. Each video can be seen as narratives of individuals with a shared identity in being able to confront a task considered daring, which is to eat something many consider to be repugnant. At the same time as they place themselves as "foodies," they are also distinguishing themselves from their viewers. Such differentiating performances will sometimes be marked by stereotypical talk which can include "other issues of power, segregation and often subjugation" (Abrahams 2003:199). For example, the use of a racializing vocabulary which serves to further "othering" or segregation into "us versus them" is evident in many of the challenge videos.

Another example of a differentiating performance is evident when Roi Fabito in his persona as "Guava Juice" reacts in a near-hysterical manner when catching a glimpse of balut. As a Filipino American who was born in the Philippines and already familiar with balut (as can be seen in a 2015 video depicting his trip to the Philippines where he also eats it, then regurgitates it back), Roi Fabito chooses to act the typical performance of disgust in making fun of balut. He asks his viewers to imagine that inside the egg is a uterus, and that "one pops the uterus" to expose "the little duckling." This choice of words serves to bring up the notion of cannibalism, an image long associated to Asian food (Ku 2013). Although in this case, Roi is from Filipino ancestry, his portrayal of the food can be interpreted as a typical Western performance. Rather than being interested in garnering cultural capital through a more nuanced appreciation of this cultural food, Roi Fabito is following the easiest way to economic capital via the use of balut as "clickbait."

In defining performance as either preserving or "reshaping" tradition, Deborah Kapchan notes that "social performances are indexes of social transformation" (2003:122). If true, what is the current state of affairs that is captured in these Balut Challenge videos? A hundred years from now, if someone was to unearth these videos which heaven forbid, may be the only thing that survived the end of this world, what could be learned from watching these?

These productions can be viewed as harbingers of the future. One, entertainment in the first two decades of the twenty-first century is now increasingly online as evident in the popularity of the videos. Six out of 10 people from the ages of 18 to 29 now prefer television via streaming services on the internet, according to a 2017 Pew Research study (Rainie 2017). Two, entertainment is more and more in compressed short bursts of time, in response to one's ever-shortening attention span.

In addition, the existence of such challenge videos is evidence that technology has developed to the point that more and more people have the capability to film high-quality videos and upload edited versions online. This means access to professional equipment and development of apps which allow such possibilities.

Instead of dying out, reality television continues to reign supreme, with shows like *The Bachelor* and *Survivor* now on its 22nd and 36th season, respectively. Their popularity can be measured in spin-offs of the shows, and others which were inspired by them. Mimicking what they see on television, people then act out their own versions in social media as can be seen in the YouTube videos which are also influenced by the experience economy.

As for the actual topic of the video, which involves challenging people to something considered a consumable and nutritious food by millions of people in Southeast Asia, that in itself speaks of the privileged lives of those in the Western half, where items that can offer beneficial sustenance to people is instead discarded, and vomited. It speaks of the prevalence of the culture of consumption where most anything can be used superficially and then disposed.

To conclude, such videos that deliberately provoke disgust as a way to earn distinction may be dismissed by some as another sign of reality television's influence, but I would like to offer some observations that may lead to another interpretation.

At first glance, these Balut Challenge videos which usually star Western performers may be accused of further "commodification of Otherness" (hooks 1992:366) as a way to earn culinary and economic capital. According to hooks, it is ethnicity which is seasoning and spice for the "dull dish that is mainstream white culture" (hooks 1992:366). Although hooks was directly examining the sexual relations between white, dominant males and non-white females as a way for the former to enter the world of "experience," to a lesser extent this also applies to eating the foods of the Other (hooks 1992:368). Eating balut would be a way to "transform" oneself, albeit a change that borders on deviation as long as the objective would be "to be changed in some way by the encounter" (hooks 1992:368).

At the same time, however, another way to interpret these videos is to see them as an example of a "reverse" colonization where a favorite street snack of millions of Filipinos is being introduced to the Western portion of the world. Whereas those privileged to indulge in haute cuisine and fine wine are thought to be influencers of what is being consumed, the fact that a food associated with the lower masses in an Asian country is now being eaten in numerous videos by relatively privileged consumers with economic access to these eggs and leisure time can be interpreted as a kind of victory. It can be seen as one example where the taste buds of Southeast Asians are shaping what is being consumed with hardly any cultural mediation.

Decontextualization and denial of the significance of the food in Philippine culture is rampant in most of these Balut Challenge videos, and there is no recognition of the racism that can be palpably felt in many of these productions which may make for a grim future where the dominated will continue to be consumed and denigrated (hooks 1992:373). Yet it is with some glee that I noted this practice of eating fertilized duck eggs is sparking interest and curiosity in the food, thereby promoting the continuing of this tradition in some fashion.

Who stands to also profit from the popularity of Balut Challenge? It is not just the performer/producer but behind the scenes, those that also benefit are duck farms and balut distributors. In addition, any mom-and-pop enterprise with a decent backyard, ducks, and access to water can produce balut, although the quality and consistency of it may vary. Small-scale as well as big-scale producers who sell balut as a sideline can also be affected favorably by the rising infamy of this food. Recognition of balut, both good and the bad, can be used as a gateway into Filipino culture as the New York restaurants of Maharlika and Jeepney have successfully demonstrated by sponsoring balut-eating contests for three years. Even after the contests were stopped, the previous deluge of publicity has assisted in cementing the recognition of the restaurants and helping to bring about the trendy Filipino food movement where Filipino chefs like Bad Saint's Tom Cunanan and restaurant owners like Nicole Ponseca are making waves toward the elevation of Filipino food in the annals of haute cuisine.

It is easy to dismiss Balut Challenge as another form of cultural food colonialism (Heldke 2003). Yet I submit that it may also be reversing that colonization. Although I do not wish to sentimentalize resistance, it has been pointed out by Heldke that the preparation and consumption of one's foodways is a kind of resistance against the colonizer (Heldke 2003:10). Bite by bite, balut may be seen as reeducating and training Western palates to accept and try new foodways. Although the majority of the reactions has been one of disgust, there are spaces for other reactions and realizations that the fertilized egg has a lot more going for it than others are willing to admit. Balut is just waiting for its proper introduction, not least of it a recognition from the Paleo diet crowd that it is in many ways the perfect food.

# Conclusion

In 2017, Pulitzer-Prize-winning food critic Jonathan Gold proclaimed in his inimitable way that Filipino food was now the "it" food, and on its way to brand recognition like Korean, Thai, and Japanese cuisine (Gold 2017). Although it may not be featured in every pop-up, food stall or acclaimed Filipino restaurant, balut has undeniably played a role in the ongoing Filipino food movement that has been on the verge for many years.

Filipino food eateries have long been in present in the United States, with the earliest diners in the 1920s and 1930s aimed at filling the stomachs (and hearts) of its farm worker clientele. These early restaurants were followed by mostly fast food and casual diners where one "pointed" to a particular dish to be served, with hardly any fine dining establishments. With only a handful of exceptions, the concept of "upscale Filipino food" did not exist until the last decade or so in the United States. The dearth in Filipino fine dining in the United States was not the case in the Philippines, where many top chefs like Nora Daza had long enjoyed an international reputation for serving top-notch Filipino cuisine.

The situation changed in 2012 when Andrew Zimmern declared that Filipino food was the next hot cuisine, the same year when the balut contest in New York first took place sponsored by Maharlika restaurant (which opened in August 2011) and Jeepney gastropub (which debuted in October 2012). The buzz around Filipino food began to get coverage in the mainstream media at the same time.

Filipino food seems to have followed the same trajectory of other "ethnic" cuisines. The food was first made available to insiders via eateries which catered to them, such as the groundbreaking Filipino cafes in the 1920s and 1930s in California, before gradually becoming known by outsiders once the group amassed a visible presence in society and in the media. But it was also due to balut's presence in eating contests reported by the press and social media that lent momentum to Filipino food being "discovered" by outsiders who want to be in the know. The negative press on balut did not deter those who flocked to Filipino restaurants like Jeepney and Maharlika, which became even more popular after the contests.

What the coverage of balut and its introduction to the rest of the world via reality shows did was to prime audiences everywhere that there was this thing called "balut," and that Filipinos ate this developed chick. The horrified reactions can be said to belong to a "canon of disgust" which drew from the legacy of racialized discourse that exoticized Asian peoples and their cultural practices, including their foods, which could be traced back to anthropological displays of indigenous tribes in the nineteenth and twentieth centuries.

The resulting publicity had its good as well as bad sides. At the same time as this negative spotlight initiated a new round of differential discourse on the foods of the Other, adding to the continuing orientalization of Filipinos and other Asian Americans, the publicity of balut as the "iconic" food of the Philippines drew the curiosity of others. The exposure encouraged some to try and explore other facets of Filipino cuisine.

Balut did for Filipinos what they didn't do for themselves. A silent minority for the most part, with its colonial history of 300 years of Spanish rule followed by half a century of American colonialism, Filipino Americans have long gained the reputation of being able to fit in without standing apart. This has been a survival mechanism that has allowed them to build lives in the new country despite discriminating exclusion laws such as the Tydings-McDuffie Act of 1934 and the Filipino Repatriation Act of 1935. With the passage of the Immigration and Nationality Act of 1965, more Filipinos and other Asian immigrants were allowed in as immigrants. With their English-speaking skills and familiarity with American ways of living due to colonialism, Filipino migrants blended in and became part of the Asian model minority stereotype which viewed Asian Americans as successfully assimilated into society due to emphasis on hard work, education, and family (see Yu 2006, for more on the stereotype).

Now that those of Filipino heritage have been counted as the second largest Asian American group in the United States, the sheer numbers are talking back. One measure of their presence is through the rise of haute cuisine Filipino restaurants in the United States, including the aforementioned Bad Saint, Ma'am Sir, and Lasa. Contrary to the mainstream perception, Filipino restaurants had always existed but like the people themselves, they had been relegated to the background and interspersed with other Asian eateries like Laotian and Cambodian restaurants which are still not found as widely as Chinese and Thai restaurants. They had existed once Filipinos had arrived and settled as immigrant workers, from the 1930s in Stockton to the *turo-turo* (point-point) eateries in Asian enclaves in the East and West Coast and cities in-between such as Columbus, Ohio (where balut was present in the 1980s) to acclaimed restaurants like Cendrillon (now Purple Yam in Brooklyn) and Rice Bar in Los Angeles. But haute cuisine featuring Filipino food was not in existence for several factors, including the reluctance of chefs to cook it. It took balut—its form, its substance, and its very striking appearance—that ushered in awareness and curiosity along with revulsion and appropriation that combined, brought mainstream awareness that there was a distinct culture and cuisine worth exploring beyond the hype. It may also have galvanized others, including those chefs trained in French culinary methods, to try and do their own representation of what is Filipino cuisine.

Once in the Filipino diaspora, this street food underwent several transformations from lowly, nutritious snack to a food that nourishes culinary citizenship. Its latest incarnation as the leading role in many a food challenge online video cements its ability to procure economic and culinary capital for the consumer via its ability to act as an effective clickbait.

Balut's journey as a favorite Philippine snack began in the duck farms of Pateros, on the shores of Laguna de Bay, where access to the once-pristine freshwater ensured that ducks laid eggs that were fertilized and warmly incubated in sacks of rice husks that may have led to sweet-tasting balut. By 2018, however, the production of balut in the Philippines is now undertaken elsewhere such as the provinces of Bulacan and Zamboanga in the Philippines.

In the United States, balut is produced in duck farms such as Metzer Farms in Gonzales, California, where it is then distributed to be sold in farmer's markets, grocery stores, and flea markets. Consumers who flock to these venues come from diverse backgrounds. As a result of balut's marketing as a natural "Viagra" by vendors and distributors such as Cayetano Araujo and

Arme Nicolas, the aphrodisiac belief and other touted health benefits of balut as good for migraines and headaches are now transmitted to other ethnic groups such as Mexican Americans.

With 1 out of every 10 Filipinos working abroad worldwide, the use of balut as a symbol of culinary nationalism owes much to a healthy dose of nostalgia experienced by those far away from home. Food acts as a tonic to deal with the stress of separation from the motherland (Mannur 2007) and eating balut can be a way of dealing with this feeling of alienation. As a result of global work flows and migration, balut can be found where many Filipino overseas workers and other Asian groups reside and work, from places such as Italy, Greenland, and the Czech Republic.

For second-generation Filipinos, balut can be utilized to be more of a tool that can assist in cultural belonging. Tasting balut and championing its use in eating contests at festivals become a way to fend off the negative portrayal of the food in conventional television and on the internet. To eat it in such diasporic public settings allows those of Filipino heritage a chance to gain temporary citizenship, via the culinary route. Eating balut can also bring them culinary capital, especially for those who consume them openly in an American venue.

Although just an unassuming snack, a street food appetizer that is not even featured in many of the finest Filipino-themed restaurants in the United States (with the exception of $4 a pop at Jeepney and Maharlika in New York), balut's presence in festivals and in the social media has helped keep Filipinos in the spotlight. It illustrates how food can be a potent symbol of one's identity. Such shows are *Fear Factor* and *Survivor* may have meant to use the fertilized egg as a scare tactic to bring in the masses, but in the end, the growing number of people aware of Filipino food beyond embryonic eggs has brought awareness, with negative and positive effects. Through this Filipino food movement, those of Filipino ancestry are attempting to subvert the cultural appropriation of foods such as balut and are now talking back and claiming their turn in the spotlight.

Demonstrating the "polysemia" of food or the capacity of food to have multiple meanings and its ability to signify the situation it is used, beyond mere nutrition (Barthes 1997), balut stands for fun drinking sessions, energizer after work or at night, and brain food for students. In the United States, it can signify being a real "Filipino" or a foreign food that can be conquered to prove culinary prowess to others, whether online or in a contest. If balut is consumed with friends and family in a social ritual, this effectively "cooks" the egg and erases its liminality as it needs cultural mediation in order for it to be consumed in the right social context (Levi-Strauss [1966] 2008).

Balut again transform itself into situation when it is used as an aphrodisiac as well as a tool of othering. Although the connection between the *aswang*, a supernatural creature and balut is not as well known as that of balut's rumored ability to be an aphrodisiac, the belief in the *aswang* continues to be widespread and aided in part by the influence of the media whether in the form of movies, newspapers, and websites (Goldstein et al. 2007).

The connection of balut to the supernatural is a belief that is not as strong and widely known as the belief that balut is an aphrodisiac for men only. Although in the 1990s, this belief seemed to be mostly with men of Filipino heritage, based on balut distributors and vendors' oral testimonies, men from other ancestries are increasingly relying on balut to bring them energy and stimulate their sexual performance.

Performing masculinity seems to be evident in the consumption of balut as a natural Viagra, for it is widely seen to be for men only to "strengthen the knees" (*pampalakas ng tuhod*). Despite the fact that balut is eaten by most everyone in the Philippines, from children to the elderly, the sick and the healthy, when it comes to eating it for its aphrodisiac qualities, men are primarily seen as the ones who benefit. Beliefs tied to balut can reveal the ways that food is utilized to include and exclude others.

In investigating the visibility of balut first in mainstream media and followed by numerous appearances in eating contests held during heritage festivals, I argue that the prominence of balut in the media and online coincided with the recognition of Filipino Americans as a distinct group of immigrants who have long been seen as invisible.

Held in various localities in the Filipino diaspora, the eating contest allows participants (and audiences) to remember their cultural traditions and learn how to practice it in a visible, grand setting in front of others. The eating contests allow Filipino Americans a chance to "authenticate" their own traditions. Through food, those of Filipino heritage get a chance to overthrow the colonial narrative about the inadequacies of their foodways and overcome the embarrassment of practicing their culture. Eating balut offers that opportunity and brings on a "spontaneous communitas" (Turner 1974) that may well be an antidote to the growing xenophobia around us.

Similar to eating contests in festivals in that the food being eaten is balut, Balut Challenge videos viewed by millions online feature the stunt aspect of competitive eating front and center. These short films are mostly produced by those who are of non-Filipino heritage and are characterized by an exploitative tone where sensationalism prevails. Such videos exemplify a form of cultural food colonialism begun by nineteenth-century explorers and artists who searched for "ever more 'remote' cultures which they could co-opt, borrow from freely and out of context, and use as the raw materials for their own efforts at creation and discovery" (Heldke 2001:78).

The use of fertilized duck eggs facilitates the procurement of culinary capital for those who perform in the videos. In eating balut, the consumer uses the performance as leverage to earn views and clicks, propelling oneself above the crowd as a culinary adventurer and omnivore. Once the balut has been consumed, those featured in the videos can be interpreted as crossing a cultural bridge, or a great divide, separating themselves from the voyeurs in their audience to being active participants in the creation of their new identity as "culinary champions." With each bite, they are "authenticated" as foodies. Although they may not be overtly pointing fingers at others who have not reached their status, they have managed to distinguish themselves. The performers in Balut Challenge videos can be seen as culinary citizens of their own virtual country where being open to eating food considered dubious is proof of their omnivorous mantra (Naccarato and Le Besco 2012:78).

At the same time, these challenge videos may also illustrate a new tradition online where the folk is a group of people bound by one common factor (Dundes [1983] 1989), which in this case is balut. The tradition being shared draw from a historical "canon of disgust" which dictates the contours of the performance. Histrionics aside, the videos are also united by the fact that the performers have all faced the "daring" act of ingesting the embryonic egg in a performance that have been indelibly inked and made available for all time. Balut video challenges exemplify how the media is appropriated by many who consume it as part of the project of the self (see Appadurai 1996).

# The future for balut: Now what?

Balut's presence in the spotlight is as much a product of reality television and celebrities as Andrew Zimmern as well as other, lesser known but equally important taste purveyors who work behind the scenes such as Nicole Ponseca who co-owns Maharlika and Jeepney restaurants in New York, and PJ Quesada, businessman and founder of the nonprofit organization Filipino Food Movement. As those who shape the availability of certain Filipino foods and products, they, along with other chef-owners who are of Filipino heritage, demonstrate the possibility that Filipino cuisine may indeed be the next haute cuisine.

This full development is something that still remains to be seen, whether Filipino cuisine can truly reach the level of success enjoyed, say, for example, by Italian restaurants in the United States. Italian cuisine only became truly a part of American culture when the table had been set to be "white" which allowed Italians to reach the level of upward mobility as the Jews (Ray 2016:98). It is difficult to see how Filipino haute cuisine could succeed in a society where Asians and other groups' foodways are still racialized, and where degrees of whiteness count.

They can, however, reach some level of success in following the uneasy formula embodied in the phrase "ethnic haute cuisine" (Ray 2016). It is a path where if one who is an immigrant desires to succeed in a culinary career in the United States, they would have to have access to the right networks and education, for there is no room in the world of culinary stardom for those who are merely seen as "ethnic cooks." For Filipino American chefs such as Charles Olalia of Rice Bar and Ma'am Sir or Chad Valencia of Lasa, the path to success follows the vaulted culinary route via apprenticeship with top Western chefs and French-influenced culinary schools. To follow their rise and to document their challenges in creating what is considered haute cuisine amid competing claims of authenticity and exoticism should be a focus of subsequent work.

In his 2018 presidential address to the Association for the Study of Food and Society, Krishnendu Ray lays the groundwork on the epistemology of joy under the guise of street vending. He criticizes how theories of taste in contemporary food studies often lead to disembodied analysis (Ray 2018). Describing street foods as a study of the "palatal pleasures of the poor," Ray calls for critical alliances across disciplines and with groups such as food vendors and the examination of their challenges and what they provide in their goods to allow for a richer, more in-depth description of what causes alienation and joy. The pursuit of the pleasures of street foods "has the potential to decolonize the field of gastronomy" and one can use street foods to begin viewing "from the bottom up."

Although the sensationalism aspect of balut seems to be what is driving most of the online videos featuring the embryonic eggs, one can also take note of the irony where a Southeast Asian street food is being consumed by many mostly in the West who have access to other kinds of foods and have the time and space to play at eating. Despite the portrayal of balut as a food to be "feared," each bite of balut is "de-colonizing" and exposing Americans to a street food that is unapologetically itself, with little room to be disguised or made "Americanized." In the end, the consumption of the egg itself allows for spaces for the continuation and the possibilities in the reinterpretation of this cultural practice in different contexts. Inclusion and openness may be an unintended side effect of Balut Challenge videos and may eventually lead to the full acceptance of Filipino cuisine.

Folklore studies have long pushed the envelope in defining "who are the folk" (Dundes [1983] 1989). Folklorists have extensively paid attention to the marginalized, applauded the mundane, and found beauty in the ordinary. But since the end of the twentieth century and continuing to the twenty-first century, the field of folkloristics along with other humanities disciplines has fallen to relentless attacks in favor of so-called hard sciences that serve the profit margin. There must be a continued effort at understanding the effects of globalization, technology, and contemporary migration in the world around us, and blindly accepting the march to capitalistic development without questioning its repercussions to humanity would accelerate the decline of civility and to continue toward isolation in politics and everyday life. Folkloristics and the study of food can assist in illuminating what defines us and our fellow human beings in the world "from the bottom up."

In this study of the unassuming street food of balut, I hope that by providing an insight to how balut has been enjoyed in its traditional contexts will lead a deeper understanding of Filipino/Filipino American culture. The use of it in the celebratory contexts such as festivals in the United States also add to its capacity as a street food to challenge notions of "exotic" and "bizarre" foods, blur the lines of separation from the "Other" and enlarge the definition of what makes an American.

I had started the book noting that it is an Asian American interpretation of a Western interpretation of an Asian cultural practice. I wanted to use balut to tell the story of how globalization and migration interact in a consumption of a street food and create new expressive culture from the old. The ways and localities where balut is found exemplify how a food can often convey contradictory meanings and functions. Balut allows its consumers to broker, create, and articulate dynamic and complex identities which are influenced by the forces of globalization, diaspora, and mass media. This work hopefully will add to the interpretation of foodways and cultural practices beyond the limitations of ethnicity-based studies and gastronomical works aligned and guided by predilections toward haute cuisine. In illuminating balut and its associated beliefs and practices, done by a diverse group united with the common factor of utilizing balut as a tool for self-expression (as well as nutrition), this work looks at the cultural implications of eating balut by those in search of "authenticating" experiences for the self.

# Appendix
# 2017 BALUT SURVEY QUESTIONS

Question 1: Name, age, occupation, ethnicity (please mention if first or second generation Filipino or another ethnicity).

Question 2: Have you eaten a fertilized egg, that is, balut? If yes, please continue survey.

Question 3: Do you know another name for balut?

Question 4: When and where did you first eat balut and how old were you?

Question 5: When and where was the last time you ate balut?

Question 6: Why do you eat balut?

Question 7: Where do you tend to eat it? For example, at home, work, parties, dinner, snack during the day?

Question 8: How do you eat it? Do you also put any seasoning or condiment on it?

Question 9: Who do you eat balut with, yourself or with others?

Question 10: Is balut good for anything (e.g., health, energy, etc.)? Please explain in detail why balut is good for according to your opinion and personal experience.

Question 11: If balut is good for something, do you think balut works?

Question 12: How often do you eat balut?

Question 13: From your experience, do you know of a specific age group that tends to eat balut in the Philippines? What about in the United States?

Question 14: What immigrant groups are you aware of eating balut?

Question 15: How do you feel after you eat balut?

Question 16: Do you know of any stories, legends, proverbs (salawikan, kasabihan), or other folklore related to balut?

Question 17: Do you know of any superstitions or supernatural beliefs about balut and eating balut?

Question 18: If balut was easily available, how often would you eat it?

Question 19: Anything else you want to share about balut?

Summaries of themes from the qualitative study responses:

- All participants stated they had it with others, mostly family. At least two liked to enjoy it by themselves.
- Most had balut as children or young adults and had balut with family or at a Filipino party.
- Most cited that they loved the taste and considered it delicious.
- Some participants said they rarely buy it but enjoy it when available or during special occasions.
- Most people like it with salt or no seasoning.
- Most participants are satisfied after eating balut.
- About half of the 31 respondents believe that balut has nutritional or energizing benefits.

# Notes

## Foreword

1 This chapter has benefited immensely from the copy edits of Stephanie Jolly without whose diligence it would have been much less readable and cluttered with errors of grammar and style.

2 Author's note: A sampling of critical food studies from folklorists include Don Yoder's (1972) article on "Folk Cookery," Brown and Mussell's edited collection on ethnic and regional foods (1984), Michael Owen Jones's (1981) volume on foodways research and food as punishment (2017), Barbara Kirshenblatt-Gimblett's article on food as a performance medium (1999), Lucy Long's *Culinary Tourism* ([1998] 2004) as well as *Food and Folklore* (2015), and Jones and Long on comfort food (2017).

3 Abrahams (2005) *Everyday Life: A Poetics of Vernacular Practices*, Philadelphia: University of Pennsylvania Press.

4 Regina Bendix (1997) *In Search of Authenticity: The Formation of Folklore Studies*, Madison: University of Wisconsin Press.

5 For instance, see Alan Warde (2016), *The Practice of Eating* for an elaboration on what he claims to be the advantages of practice theory (over numerous other current theoretical frameworks): it pays attention to unconscious activities as much as ideas and norms, which is where cooking and eating register most significantly; it avoids the twin errors of individualism and holism where everything is reduced either to individual choice or full structural determinism; it can accommodate sayings and doings without falling into discourse analysis or unthinking acts; it can explain how everyday activities such as shopping, cooking, and eating can be both regular, un-thought and yet normatively regulated activities; and finally, a practice framework can accommodate continuity and change in cooking and eating practices. The result of excessive individual-rational decision-making about matters that should legitimately be the ambit of communities of practice is delineated by Claude Fischler in his 1988 essay as anomie and normlessness, titled "Food, Self, and Identity," *Social Science Information*, 27 (2): 275–292.

6  Fernandez (2003:61–71, 64).

7  Patel and Moore (2017:45) in *A History of the World in Seven Cheap Things*. Oakland: University of California Press.

8  To use Robert Ji-Song Ku's felicitous phrase in 2013, *Dubious Gastronomy: The Cultural Politics of Eating Asian in the USA*. Honolulu: University of Hawai'i Press.

# Chapter 2

1  The word "maharlika" refers to an ancient class of noble and aristocratic people in pre-Hispanic Philippines.

# Chapter 3

1  Simon Bronner in his 1981 article noted paradoxical food-related behaviors, "The Paradox of Pride and Loathing, and Other Problems," *Western Folklore* 40 (1), Foodways and Eating Habits: Directions for Research (1981), 115–124. Bronner questioned why people continue to eat certain foods they do not enjoy or find hard to prepare yet it remains a prominent part of their culture.

2  Although most of my respondents did not identify a connection between balut and the belief in the *aswang*, psychoanalytical folklorist Alan Dundes argued that folklore is the expression of the unconscious so most people would not be aware of the meaning of their lore (Dundes 1976, 1980).

3  For a background in psychosexuality and the oral stage, see Freud (1905).

# Chapter 4

1  Folklorists have extensively studied the genre of festivals, including Bauman and Abrahams (1978); Bauman and Stoeltje (1989); Magliocco (1993); Santino (1994), and Dundes and Falassi (1975).

2  Arnold Van Gennep in 1909 identified the three stages in a rite-of-passage, with the first phase referring to separation where one is removed from a former status, to the second stage of liminality where one is isolated from others in the community, and to the final stage of incorporation to the group as a member with a new status.

3  Liminal can be defined as an indefinite threshold where one is not incorporated or transitioned to the next rite or stage in life (Van Gennep 1909; also see Turner 1967).

4  Turner defined three types of communitas: spontaneous, ideological, and normative. "Spontaneous communitas is 'a direct, immediate and total confrontation of human identities,' a deep rather than intense style of personal interaction" with a "magical" quality to it (1974:79). Ideological communitas is defined as theorizing or analyzing spontaneous communitas, a "retrospective" which serves to distance the individual from the immediate experience while normative communitas is when a group tries to sustain spontaneous communitas beyond its temporary status, by legislating into being, as can be seen during "religious revivals" (Turner 1974:79–81).

5  See Von Sydow (1977:44–59). Von Sydow also discussed "passive bearers" or those who know of a tradition but do not transmit it.

# Chapter 5

1  See, for example, Fernandez and Alegre (1988), Fernandez (1996a, 1996b).

2  Durian is a creamy, sweet, and savory-tasting fruit eaten commonly in Southeast Asia, which when ripened, has a unique odor that has been described as "skunky" and "metallic" (Stromberg 2012). Other descriptions note the fruit's scent to be "a penetrating aroma of vanilla, rotten eggs, almonds, turpentine, and old shoes" (Kirshenblatt-Gimblett 1999). For Western attitudes toward the fruit as an exoticized food in colonial Southeast Asia, see Montanari (2017).

3  Face-to-face communication and orality have commonly been part of defining what is folklore, but as Dundes and Pagter (1975) have illustrated, these do not need to be present in order for expressive culture to occur.

# References

Abalos, J. (2011), "Determinants of Men's Extramarital Sexual Experience in the Philippines," *Philippine Population Review*, 10 (2): 51–74. Available online: https://www.researchgate.net/publication/313438627 (accessed July 18, 2017).

Abrahams, R. (1984), "Equal Opportunity Eating: A Structural Excursus on Things of the Mouth," in L. K. Brown and K. Mussell (eds), *Ethnic and Regional Foodways in the United States: The Performance of Group Identity*, 19–36, Knoxville: University of Tennessee.

Abrahams, R. (2003), "Identity," in B. Feintuch (ed.), *Eight Words for the Study of Expressive Culture*, 198–222, Chicago: University of Illinois Press. Available online: http://www.jstor.org/stable/10.5406/j.ctt2ttc8f.12 (accessed September 15, 2017).

Abrahams, R. (2005) *Everyday Life: A Poetics of Vernacular Practices*, Philadelphia: University of Pennsylvania Press.

Alegado, D. T. (1992), "The Political Economy of International Labor Migration from the Philippines," dissertation, University of Hawai'i, Manoa, Honolulu.

Anderson, A. (1998), "Cosmopolitanism, Universalism, and the Divided Legacies of Modernity," in P. Cheah and B. Robbins (eds), *Cosmopolitics: Thinking and Feeling beyond the Nation*, 265–289, Minneapolis and London: University of Minnesota.

Anderson, B. ([1983] 1991), *Imagined Communities: Reflections on the Origin and Spread of Nationalism*, London: Verso.

Anderson, J. A. (1971), "The Study of Contemporary Foodways in American Folklife Research," *Keystone Folklore*, 16: 155–163.

Andres, T. (1987), *Understanding the Filipino*, Manila: Cellar Book Shop.

Andres, T. (1994), *Dictionary of Filipino Culture and Values*, Quezon City: Giraffe Books.

Appadurai, A. (1988), "How to Make a National Cuisine: Cookbooks in Contemporary India," *Comparative Studies in Society and History*, 30: 3–24.

Appadurai, A. (1996), *Modernity at Large: Cultural Dimensions of Globalization (Public Worlds, Vol. 1) 1st Edition*, Minneapolis: University of Minnesota Press.

Appiah, K. A. (2019), "The Importance of Elsewhere. In Defense of Cosmopolitanism," *Foreign Affairs*, March–April issue. Available online: https://www.foreignaffairs.com/articles/2019-02-12/importance-elsewhere (accessed February 23, 2019).

Asis, M. (2017), "The Philippines: Beyond Labor Migration, toward Development and (Possibly) Return," *Migration Policy Institute*, July 12. Available online:

https://www.migrationpolicy.org/article/philippines-beyond-labor-migration-toward-development-and-possibly-return (accessed May 15, 2018).

*The Aswang Phenomenon* (2011), [Film] Dir. Jordan Clark, Canada: High Banks.

Augustyn, A. (2018), "Survivor: American Television Show," *Encyclopedia Britannica*. Available online: https://www.britannica.com/topic/Survivor-American-television-show (accessed February 2, 2018).

Ault, A. (2017), "'Are Oysters an Aphrodisiac?' Sure, If You Think So," Smithsonian.com, February 13. Available online: https://www.smithsonianmag.com/smithsonian-institution/are-oysters-aphrodisiac-180962148/#J24lZ6RoLdOzbx tq.99 (accessed May 21, 2018).

Azurin, A. (1995), *Reinventing the Filipino Sense of Being and Becoming: Critical Analyses of the Orthodox Views in Anthropology, History, Folklore & Letters 2nd edition*, Diliman: University of the Philippines Press.

Barthes, R. (1997), "Toward a Psychosociology of Contemporary Food Consumption," in C. Counihan and P. V. Esterik (eds), *Food and Culture: A Reader*, 20–27, New York: Routledge.

Bauman, R. (1974), "Verbal Art as Performance," *American Anthropologist*, 77 (2): 290–311.

Bauman, R. and R. Abrahams (1978), "Ranges of Festival Behavior," in B. Babcock (ed.), *The Reversible World: Inversion in Art and Society*, 193–207, Ithaca, NY: Cornell University Press.

Bauman, R. and B. Stoeltje (1989), "Community Festival and the Enactment of Modernity," in R. E. Walls and G. Schoemaker (eds), *The Old Traditional Way of Life: Essays in Honor of Warren E. Roberts*, 158–171, Bloomington, IN: Trickster Press.

Bayoran, G. (2009), "Raps Filed vs. Self-Confessed Killer," *The Visayan Daily Star*, July 4. Available online: http://www.archives.visayandailystar.com/2009/July/04/topstory9.htm (accessed May 24, 2018).

Beit-Hallahmi, B. (1985), "Dangers of the Vagina," *British Journal of Medical Psychology*, 58: 351–356.

Ben-Amos, D. (1971), "Toward New Perspectives in Folklore," *Journal of American Folklore*, 84 (331): 3–15.

Ben-Amos, D. ([1969] 1976), "Analytical Categories and Ethnic Genres," in *Folklore Genres*, 215–242, Austin: University of Texas. Available online: http://www.jstor.org/stable/10.7560/724150.16 (accessed January 24, 2018).

Bendix, R. (1997), *In Search of Authenticity*, Madison: University of Wisconsin.

Bendix, R. and M. Fenske, eds (2014), *Politische Mahlzeiten. Political Meals*, Berlin: LIT Verlag Münster.

Benedek, T. (1972), "Food and Drink as Aphrodisiacs," *Sexual Behavior*, 2: 5–10.

Besa, A. and R. Dorotan (2006), *Memories of Philippine Kitchens: Stories and Recipes from Far and Near*, New York: Stewart, Tabori & Chang.

Blank, T., ed. (2009), *Folklore and the Internet: Vernacular Expression in a Digital World*, Logan: Utah State University Press.

Bourdieu, P. ([1979] 1984), *Distinction: A Social Critique of the Judgement of Taste*, trans. R. Nice, London and New York: Routledge.

Bourdieu, P. ([1983] 1986), "Forms of Capital," in J. Richardson (ed.), *Handbook of Theory of Research for the Sociology of Education*, 241–258, Westport, CT: Greenwood.

Bronner, S. J. (1981), "The Paradox of Pride and Loathing, and Other Problems," *Western Folklore*, 40 (1): 115–124.

Bronner, S. J. (2009), "Digitizing and Virtualizing Folklore," in T. Blank (ed.), *Folklore and the Internet: Vernacular Expression in a Digital World*, 21–66, Logan: Utah State University Press.

Brown, L. K. and K. Mussell (1984), *Ethnic and Regional Foodways in the United States: The Performance of Group Identity*, Knoxville: University of Tennessee.

Buchholdt, T. (1996), *Filipinos in Alaska, 1788–1958*, Anchorage: Aboriginal Press.

Burns, L. M. (2013), *Puro Arte: Filipinos on the Stages of Empire*, New York and London: New York University Press.

Burton, R. and F. F. Arbuthnot ([1886] 1988), *The Kama Sutra [Vatsyanyana]. The Perfumed Garden [Cheikh Nefzaoui]*, London: Bibliophile Books.

Cabotaje, E. M. (1976), *Food and Philippine Culture: A Study in Culture and Education*, Manila: Centro Escolar University.

Calvert, A. (2014), "You Are What You (M)eat: Explorations of Meat-Eating, Masculinity and Masquerade," *Journal of International Women's Studies*, 16 (1): 18–33.

Camp, C. (1980), "Foodways," Vol. 2, in M. T. Inge (ed.), *Handbook of American Popular Culture*, 141–161, Westport, CT: Greenwood Press.

Camp, C. (1989), *American Foodways: What, When, Why and How We Eat in America*, Little Rock: August House.

Chang, H. C. and C. Dagaas (2004), "The Philippine Duck Industry: Issues and Research Needs," *Working Paper Series in Agricultural and Resource Economics, University of New England Graduate School of Agricultural and Resource Economics & School of Economics*, 1: 1–31. Available online: http://ageconsearch.umn.edu/bitstream/12904/1/wp040001.pdf (accessed August 12, 2017).

Claudio, V. S. (1994), *Filipino American Food Practices, Customs, & Holidays*, Chicago, IL: American Dietetic Association.

Cordero-Fernando, G. (1992), *Philippine Food and Life: Luzon*, Manila: Anvil Publishing.

Crawfurd, J. (1830), *Journal of an Embassy from the Governor-General of India to the Courts of Siam and Cochin China; Exhibiting a View of the Actual State of Those Kingdoms*, 2nd edition, Vol. 1 of 2, London: Henry Colburn & Richard Bentley.

Cuaresma, B. (2018), "OFW Remittances Hit $28.1 Billion in 2017," *Business Mirror*, February 15. Available online: https://businessmirror.com.ph/2018/02/15/ofw-remittances-hit-28-1-billion-in-2017/ (accessed January 12, 2019).

De Guzman, N. (2017), "There Are No More Patos in Pateros," *Business World*, February 16. Available online: http://bworldonline.com/there-are-no-more-patos-in-paternos (accessed May 2, 2018).

De Jesus, M. K. (1986), *Folk Culture of the Central Visayas*, Kalinangan Series 2, Manila: Ministry of Education, Culture & Sports, Philippines.

Demetrio, F. (1971), *Dictionary of Philippine Folk Beliefs and Customs*, 4 vols., Cagayan de Oro City, Philippines: Xavier University Press.

DeSoucey, M. (2010), "Gastronationalism: Food Traditions and Authenticity Politics in the European Union," *American Sociological Review*, 75: 432.

Douglas, M. (1966), *Purity and Danger. An Analysis of Concepts of Pollution and Taboo*, New York: Praeger Publishers.

Dundes, A. (1965), "What Is Folklore?," in A. Dundes (ed.), *The Study of Folklore*, 1–3, New Jersey: Prentice Hall.

Dundes, A. (1968), "The Number Three in American Culture," in A. Dundes (ed.), *Every Man His Own Way: Readings in Cultural Anthropology*, 401–424, Ann Arbor: University of Michigan.

Dundes, A. (1976), "Projection in Folklore: A Plea for Psychoanalytic Semiotics," *Comparative Literature*, 91 (6): 1500–1533.

Dundes, A. (1980), *Interpreting Folklore*, Bloomington: Indiana University Press.

Dundes, A. ([1983] 1989), "Defining Identity through Folklore," in A. Dundes (ed.), *Folklore Matters*, 1–39, Knoxville: University of Tennessee.

Dundes, A. and A. Falassi (1975), *La Terra in Piazza: An Interpretation of the Palio in Siena*, Berkeley: University of California Press.

Dundes, A. and C. Pagter (1975), *Work Hard and You Shall Be Rewarded. Urban Folklore from the Paperwork Empire*, Detroit: Wayne University Press.

Duval, M. (1885), "Sur les oeufs pourris comme aliment en Chine," *Bulletins de la Societe D'Anthropologie de Paris*, troisieme serie, 8: 209–300.

Espina, M. (1988), *Filipinos in Louisiana*, New Orleans: A. F. Laborde & Sons.

Eviota, E. (1992), *The Political Economy of Gender. Women and the Sexual Division of Labour in the Philippines*, London and New Jersey: Zed Books Ltd.

Falassi, A. (1987), *Time Out of Time: Essays on the Festival*, Albuquerque: University of New Mexico.

Ferguson, P. (2010), "Culinary Nationalism," *Gastronomica*, 10 (1): 102–109. Available online: https://www.researchgate.net/publication/51094981 (accessed March 16, 2017).

Fernandez, D. and E. Alegre (1988), *Sarap: Essays on Philippine Food*, Aduana, Intramuros, Manila: Mr. & Mrs. Publishing Company.

Fernandez, D. G. (1994), *Tikim: Essays on Philippine Food and Culture*, Pasig: Anvil Publishing.

Fernandez, D. (1996a), "The Taste of the Perfect 'Balut,'" *Philippine Daily Inquirer*, August 27.

Fernandez, D. G. (1996b), "The World of Balut," *Food*, September 10–12.

Fernandez, D. (2002), "Food and War," in A. Velasco Shaw and L. H. Francia (eds), *Vestiges of War: The Philippine-American War and the Aftermath of an Imperial Dream 1899-1999*, 237–246, New York: New York University Press.

Fernandez, D. G. (2003), "Culture Ingested: Notes on the Indigenization of Philippine Food," *Gastronomica*, 3 (1): 61–71.

Fernandez, D. G. (2005), "Food in the Philippines: Islands with a History of Colonization Nourished a People with a Gift for Adaptation," in R. Alejandro (ed.), *The Food of the Philippines*, 5–7, Singapore: Periplus Editions.

Francia, L. H. (2010), *A History of the Philippines: From Indios Bravos to Filipinos*, New York: The Overlook Press, 2010.

Frazer, J. (1935), *The Golden Bough: A Study in Magic and Religion*, 3rd edition, Vol. 1 of 12, New York: The Macmillan Co.

Frazier, J. (1970), *Aphrodisiac Cookery, Ancient and Modern*, San Francisco, CA: Troubadour Press.

Freud, S. ([1905] 2016), *Three Essays on the Theory of Sexuality: The 1905 Edition by Sigmund Freud*, trans. U. Kistner, eds P. Van Haute and H. Westerink, London and New York: Verso.

Garcia, M. (1979), *Readings in Philippine Prehistory*, Manila: The Filipiniana Book Guild.

Georges, R. A. (1984), "You Often Eat What Others Think You Are: Food as an Index of Others' Conceptions of Who One Is," *Western Folklore*, 43: 249–255.

Gold, J. (2017), "Jonathan Gold Says the Time for Filipino Cuisine Is Now, and the Place Is Los Angeles," *Los Angeles Times*, May 19. Available online: http://www.latimes.com/food/la-fo-filipino-cuisine-20170511-story.html (accessed May 19, 2017).

Goldstein, D. (2007), "Scientific Rationalism and Supernatural Experience Narratives," in D. Goldstein, S. A. Grider and J. B. Thomas (eds), *Haunting

*Experiences: Ghosts in Contemporary Folklore*, 60–78, Logan: Utah State University Press.

Goldstein, D., S. A. Grider and J. B. Thomas, eds (2007), *Haunting Experiences: Ghosts in Contemporary Folklore*, Logan: Utah State University Press.

Gomez, C. (2014), "Man Beheads Mother, Claims She's an 'Aswang,'" Inquirer.net, July 24. Available online: http://newsinfo.inquirer.net/623117/man-beheads-mother-claims-shes-an-aswang#ixzz5LNfX9T6P (accessed June 18, 2017).

Gonsalves, T. S. and R. N. Labrado (2011), *Filipinos in Hawaii*, Charleston, South Carolina: Arcadia Publishing.

Gonzalez-Tabujara, M. (1985), *Visayan Folklore*, Diliman, Quezon City: University of the Philippines.

Goode, J., J. Theophano and K. Curtis (1984), "A Framework for the Analysis of Continuity and Change in Shared Social Cultural Rules for Food Use: The Italian-American Pattern," in L. K. Brown and K. Mussell (eds), *Ethnic and Regional Foodways in the United States, The Performance of Group Identity*, 66–88, Knoxville: The University of Tennessee Press.

Goodland, R. (1931), *A Bibliography of Sex Rites & Customs*, London: Routledge & Sons.

Gonzalez III, J. J. (2012), *Diaspora Diplomacy. Philippine Migration and Its Soft Power Influences*, Minneapolis, MN: Mill City Press.

Grindstaff, B. (1999), "Creating Identity: Exhibiting the Philippines at the 1904 Louisiana Purchase Exposition," *National Identities*, 1 (3): 245–263. Available online: https://www.tandfonline.com/doi/abs/10.1080/14608944.1999.9728114 (accessed May 24, 2016).

Gutierrez, C. P. (1984), "The Social and Symbolic Uses of Ethnic/Regional Foodways: Cajuns and Crawfish in South Louisiana," in L. Brown and K. Mussell (eds), *Ethnic and Regional Foodways in the United* States. *The Performance of Group Identity*, 169–182, Knoxville: University of Tennessee Press.

Halloran, V. N. (2004), "Biting Reality: Extreme Eating and the Fascination with the Gustatory Abject," *Iowa Journal of Cultural Studies*, 4: 27–43.

Harris-Lopez, T. (2003), "Genre," in B. Feintuch (ed.), *Eight Words for the Study of Expressive Culture*, 99–120. Available online: http://www.jstor.org/stable/10.5406/j.ctt2ttc8f.8 (accessed November 1, 2017).

Heisley, D. D. (1990), "Gender Symbolism in Food," dissertation, Northwestern University.

Heldke, L. (2001), "'Let's Eat Chinese!': Reflections on Cultural Food Colonialism," *Gastronomica*, 1 (2): 76–79. Available online: http://www.jstor.org/stable/10.1525/gfc.2001.1.2.76 (accessed November 1, 2017).

Heldke, L. (2003), *Exotic Appetites: Ruminations of a Food Adventurer*, New York and London: Routledge.

Hendrickson, R. (1974), *Lewd Food: The Complete Guide to Aphrodisiac Edibles*, Radnor, PA: Chilton Book Co.

hooks, b. (1992), "Eating the Other: Desire and Resistance," in b. hooks (ed.), *Black Looks: Race and Representation*, 21–39, Boston, MA: South End Press.

Humphrey, T. C. and L. Humphrey, eds (1988), "*We Gather Together*": Food and Festival in American Life, Logan: Utah State University Press.

Hufford, D. (1982), *The Terror That Comes in the Night: An Experience-Centered Study of Supernatural Assault Traditions*, Philadelphia: University of Pennsylvania.

Ibanez, Florante Peter and Roselyn Estepa Ibanez (2009), *Filipinos in Carson and the South Bay*, San Francisco, CA: Arcadia.

Ileto, R. (1979), *Pasyon and Revolution: Popular Movements in the Philippines, 1840–1910*, Quezon City: Ateneo de Manila Press.

Ileto, R. (2002), "The Philippine-American War: Friendship and Forgetting," in A. Velasco Shaw and L. H. Francia (eds), *Vestiges of War: The Philippine-American War and the Aftermath of an Imperial Dream 1899–1999*, 3–21, New York: New York University Press.

Isaac, A. P. (2006), *American Tropics: Articulating Filipino America*, Minneapolis: University of Minnesota Press.

Jenks, A. E. (1905), *The Bontoc Igorot*, Manila: Bureau of Public Printing.

Jocano, F. L. (1975a), *The Philippines at the Spanish Contact*, Manila: MCS Enterprises.

Jocano, F. L. (1975b), *Philippine Prehistory. An Anthropological Overview of the Beginnings of Filipino Society and Culture*, Diliman: Philippine Center for Advanced Studies.

Johnston, J. and S. Baumann (2010), *Foodies: Democracy and Distinction in the Gourmet Foodscape*, New York: Routledge.

Jones, M. O., ed. (1981), *Western Folklore Special Issue—Foodways and Eating Habits: Directions for Research*, Los Angeles: California Folklore Society.

Jones, M. O. (2000), "What's Disgusting, Why, and What Does It Matter?," *Journal of Folklore Research*, 37 (1): 53–71.

Jones, M. O. (2005), "Food Choice, Symbolism, and Identity: Bread and Butter Issues for Folkloristics and Nutrition Studies," *Journal of American Folklore*, 120 (476): 129–177. Available online: https://doi.org/10.1353/jaf.2007.0037 (accessed May 17, 2018).

Jones, M. O. (2017), "Eating behind Bars: On Punishment, Resistance, Policy, and Applied Folkloristics," *Journal of American Folklore*, 13 (515): 72–108. Available online: www.jstor.org/stable/10.5406/jamerfolk.130.515.0072 (accessed May 2, 2018).

Jones, M. O. and L. Long, eds (2017), *Comfort Food: Meanings and Memories*, Jackson: University Press of Mississippi.

José, F. S. (1992), *Dusk*, New York: Random House.

Julian (2018), "How Much Money Guava Juice Makes on YouTube—Net Worth," Nailbuzz.com, January 9. Available online: https://naibuzz.com/much-money-guava-juice-makes-youtube (accessed May 12, 2018).

Kalcik, S. (1984), "Ethnic Foodways in America: Symbol and the Performance of Identity," in L. K. Brown and K. Mussell (eds), *Ethnic and Regional Foodways in the United States: The Performance of Group Identity*, 37–65, Knoxville: University of Tennessee.

Kapchan, D. (2003), "Performance," in B. Feintuch (ed.), *Eight Words for the Study of Expressive Culture*, 121–145, Chicago: University of Illinois Press. Available online: http://www.jstor.org/stable/10.5406/j.ctt2ttc8f.9 (accessed May 22, 2018).

Kaufman, F. (2009), *A Short History of the American Stomach*, Wilmington, MA: First Mariner Books.

Kilham, C. (2011), "Eating Balut: Going Too Far?," Fox News Health, September 15. Available online: http://www.foxnews.com/health/2011/09/12/eating-balut-going-too-far.html (accessed May 2, 2017).

Kirshenblatt Gimblett, B. (1991), "Course Outline: Food and Performance," *Digest*, 11 (1–2): 11–17, 26.

Kirshenblatt Gimblett, B. (1999), "Playing to the Senses: Food as a Performance Medium," *Performance Research: A Journal of the Performing Arts*, 4 (1): 1–30. Available online: https://doi.org/10.1080/13528165.1999.10871639 (accessed March 12, 2017).

Karnow, S. (1989), *In Our Image: America's Empire in the Philippines*, New York: Ballantine Books.

Koerner, M. R. (2007), *Filipinos in Los Angeles*, San Francisco, CA: Arcadia Publishing, 2007.

Ku, R. Ji-Song (2013), *Dubious Gastronomy: The Cultural Politics of Eating Asian in the USA*, Honolulu: University of Hawai'i Press.

Ku, R. Ji-Song, M. F. Manalansan IV and A. Mannur, eds (2013), *Eating Asian America*, New York and London: New York University Press.

Law, L. (2001), "Home Cooking: Filipino Women and Geographies of the Senses in Hong Kong," *Ecumene*, 8 (3): 264–283.

Legman, G. (1969), *Oragenitalism: Oral Techniques in Genital Excitation*, New York: The Julian Press.

Leung, W., R. Butrun and F. Chang (1972), *Food Composition Table for Use in East Asia*, Part 1. DHEW Publication No. (NIH) 73–465, Bethesda: U.S. Dept. of Health, Education and Welfare and the Food and Agricultural Organization of the United Nations.

Levi-Strauss, C. (1966), "The Culinary Triangle," *Partisan Review*, 33: 586–595.

Lieban, R. (1967), *Cebuano Sorcery: Malign Magic in the Philippines*, Berkeley: University of California Press.

Lockwood, Y. R. and W. G. Lockwood (1998), "Pasties in Michigan's Upper Peninsula: Foodways, Interethnic Relations, and Regionalism," in B. G. Shortridge and J. R. Shortridge (eds), *The Taste of American Place. A Reader on Regional and Ethnic Foods*, 21–36, Lanham: Rowman & Littlefield Publishers, Inc.

Lockwood, W. G. and Y. Lockwood (2000), "Continuity and Adaptation in Arab American Foodways," in N. Abraham and A. Shyrock (eds), *Arab Detroit: From Margin to Mainstream*, 515–549, Detroit: Wayne State University.

Lohman, S. (2016), "Pie Fight: A Brief History of Competitive Eating," *Lapham's Quarterly*, November 22. Available online: https://www.laphamsquarterly.org/roundtable/pie-fight (accessed September 30, 2017).

Long, L. (2004), "Introduction," in L. Long (ed.), *Culinary Tourism*, 1–19, Lexington: University of Kentucky Press.

Long, L. (2009), "Introduction," *Journal of American Folklore*, 122 (483): 3–10. Available online: https://www.jstor.org/stable/20487643 (accessed May 17, 2017).

Long, L., ed. (2015), "General Introduction," in L. Long (ed.), *The Food and Folklore Reader*, 1–5, London and New York: Bloomsbury.

Lopez, Mellie (1986), *A Study of Philippine Folklore*, published dissertation, University of California, Berkeley.

Lopez, Meneil (2014), "'Aswang' Killed by Neighbor in Bacolod City," ABS-CBN News Negros, September 4. Available online: http://news.abs-cbn.com/nation/regions/09/04/14/aswang-killed-neighbor-bacolod-city (accessed July 15, 2018).

Mabalon, D. (2013), "As American as Jackrabbit Adobo. Cooking, Eating, and Becoming Filipina/o American before World War II," in R. Ku, M. F. Manalansan and A. Mannur (eds), *Eating Asian America*, 147–176, New York and London: New York University Press.

Mabalon, D. and R. Reyes (2008), *Images of America. Filipinos in Stockton*, Charleston, South Carolina: Arcadia Publishing.

Magat, M. (2002), "Balut: Fertilized Duck Eggs and Their Role in Filipino Culture," *Western Folklore*, 61: 63–96.

Magat, M. (2003), "Transnational Lives, Cosmopolitan Women: Filipina Domestic Workers and Expressive Culture in Rome, Italy," Phd. dissertation, University of Pennsylvania, Philadelphia.

Magat, M. (2013), "Follow That Cheese: Tracing the Evolution of Queso de bola or Edam Cheese and Its Consumption and Role in Filipino and Filipino American Practices," unpublished paper, *American Folklore Society*, Providence, Rhode Island, October 16.

Magat, M. (2015), "Philippines," in L. Long (ed.), *Ethnic American Food Today*, 500–507, New York: Rowman and Littlefield.

Magliocco, S. (1993), "Playing with Food: The Negotiation of Identity in the Ethnic Display Event by Italian Americans in Clinton, Indiana," in L. D. Guidice (ed.), *Studies in Italian American Folklore*, 107–126, Logan: Utah State University.

Manalansan, M. (2013), "Beyond Authenticity: Rerouting the Filipino Culinary Diaspora," in R. Ji-Song Ku, M. Manalansan IV and A. Mannur (eds), *Eating Asian America: A Food Studies Reader*, 288–300, New York: New York University Press.

Maness, H. (1950), "Balut—a Duck Egg Delicacy," *World's Poultry Science Journal*, 6: 10–13.

Mannur, A. (2007), "Culinary Nostalgia. Authenticity, Nationalism, and Diaspora," *MELUS*, 32 (4): 11–31.

Mariano, H. ([1933] 1972), "The Filipino Immigrants in the U.S.," MA thesis, University of Oregon, San Francisco: R and E Research Associates.

Matejowsky, T. (2007), "SPAM and Fast-Food 'Glocalization' in the Philippines," *Food, Culture & Society*, 10 (1): 23–41. Available online: https://doi.org/10.2752/155280107780154088 (accessed January 2, 2019).

Matejowsky, T. (2013), "The Incredible, Edible Balut: Ethnographic Perspectives on the Philippines' Favorite Liminal Food," *Food, Culture & Society*, 16 (3): 387–404.

Mazereeuw, R. (2017), "How Does the YouTube Algorithm Work? A Guide to Getting More Views," *Hootsuite*, August 3. Available online: https://blog.hootsuite.com/how-the-youtube-algorithm-works/ (accessed May 21, 2018).

Melendy, H. B. (1981), *Asians in America: Filipinos, Koreans, and East Indians*, New York: Hippocrene Books.

Menez, H. (1996), *Explorations in Philippine Folklore*, Quezon City: Ateneo de Manila Press.

Mishan, L. (2018), "Filipino Food Finds a Place in American Mainstream," *New York Times*, March 12. Available online: https://www.nytimes.com/2018/03/12/dining/filipino-cooking.html (accessed January 3, 2019).

Montanari, A. (2017), "The Stinky King: Western Attitudes toward the Durian in Colonial Southeast Asia," *Food, Culture & Society*, 20 (3): 395–414.

Mydans, S. (1997), "The World: The Philippines—What the World Eats While It Watches; the Snacks Are Here: Duck!," *New York Times*, January 26, section 4, column 4: 3.

Naccarato, P. and K. Lebesco (2012), *Culinary Capital*, London and New York: Berg.

Navarrete, R. (2011), "Balut & Fear Factor," online video clip. YouTube, June 24. Available online: https://www.youtube.com/watch?v=YwfXK9s7VFQ (accessed June 1, 2017).

National Broadcasting News (2014), "On a mission to spread Filipino food, balut takes center stage", September 24. Available online: https://www.nbcnews. com/news/asian-america/mission-spread-filipino-food-balut-takes-center-stage-n208666 (accessed May 1, 2017).

Newall, V. (1971), *An Egg at Easter: A Folklore Study*, Bloomington: Indiana University Press.

Orquiza Jr., R. (2013), "Lechon with Heinz, Lea & Perrins with Adobo. The American Relationship with Filipino Food, 1898–1946," in R. Ji-Song Ku, M. F. Manalansan IV and A. Mannur (eds), *Eating Asian America*, 147–176, New York and London: New York University Press.

Otero, S. (1996), "Fearing Our Mothers: An Overview of the Psychoanalytic Theories Concerning the Vagina Dentata Motif F547.1.1.," *American Journal of Psychoanalysis*, 56: 269–288.

Parreñas, R. S. (1998), "'White Trash' Meets the 'Little Brown Monkeys': The Taxi Dance Hall as a Site of Interracial and Gender Alliances between White Working Class Women and Filipino Immigrant Men in the 1920s and 30s," *Amerasia Journal*, 24 (2): 115–134.

Pastor, C. (2015a), "Pinoy Resto Owners in NY Divided over Having 'Balut' on Their Menus," *GMA News Online*, May 7. Available online: http://www.gmanetwork. com/news/news/pinoyabroad/483202/pinoy-resto-owners-in-ny-divided-over-having-balut-on-their-menus/story (accessed June 15, 2017).

Pastor, C. D. (2015b), "Chefs Rally behind Restaurant Week, but Divided over 'Balut' and Notion of What Makes Filipino Food Special," *The FilAm*, May 6. Available online: http://thefilam.net/archives/18132 (accessed May 3, 2017).

Patel, R. and and J. Moore (2017), *A History of the World in Seven Cheap Things*, Oakland: University of California Press.

Pido, A. (1997), "Macro, Micro Dimensions of Pilipino Immigration to the United States," in M. Root (ed.), *Filipino Americans: Transformation and Identity*, 21–38, Thousand Oaks, CA: Sage Publications.

Piers Morgan Live (2013), [TV programme], Bourdain Eats Fetal Duck Egg on the Air, CNN.com, April 11, 21.00.

Pilcher, J. M. (1998), *Que Vivan Los Tamales!: Food and the Making of Mexican Identity*, Albuquerque: University of New Mexico.

Pinoy, P. (2015), "Filipino New Yorkers to Animal Rights Activists: 'Leave Our Balut Alone!'," *Adobo Chronicles*, April 18. Available online: http://adobochronicles.com/2015/04/18/filipino-new-yorkers-to-animal-rights-activists-leave-our-balut-alone (accessed June 21, 2015).

Pollan, M. (2006), *The Omnivore's Dilemma: A Natural History of Four Meals*, New York: Penguin Books.

Ponce de Leon, J. (2016), "Filipino Delicacy Balut Not Allowed in Luggage to UAE," *Gulf News*, June 7. Available online: http://gulfnews.com/news/uae/society/filipino-delicacy-balut-not-allowed-in-luggage-to-uae-1.1841922 (accessed July 30, 2017).

Postma, A. (1992), "Philippines. The Laguna Copper-Plate Inscription: Text and Commentary," *Philippine Studies*, 40 (2): 183–203.

Rafael, V. (2000), *White Love and Other Events in Filipino History*, Durham, NC and London: Duke University Press.

Rafael, V. (2002), "Parricides, Bastards and Counterrevolution: Reflections on the Philippine Centennial," in A. Velasco Shaw and L. H. Francia (eds), *Vestiges of War: The Philippine-American War and the Aftermath of an Imperial Dream 1899–1999*, 361–375, New York: New York University Press.

Rainie, L. (2017), "About 6 in 10 Young Adults in U.S. Primarily Use Online Streaming to Watch TV," *Pew Research Center*, September 13. Available online: http://www.pewresearch.org/fact-tank/2017/09/13/about-6-in-10-young-adults-in-u-s-primarily-use-online-streaming-to-watch-tv/ (accessed May 31, 2018).

Ramos, M. (1969), "The Aswang Syncrasy in Philippine Folklore," *Western Folklore*, 28 (1969): 238–248.

Ramos, M. (1971), *Creatures of Lower Philippine Mythology*, Manila: University of the Philippines Press.

Ramos, M. (1973), *Filipino Cultural Patterns and Values and Their Mythological Dimensions*, Diliman: Island Publishers.

Ramos, M. (1990a), *Philippine Demonological Legends and Their Cultural Bearings*, Quezon City: Phoenix Publishing House.

Ramos, M. (1990b), *The Aswang Complex in Philippine Folklore*, Quezon City: Phoenix Publishing House.

Rappler (2015), "Should a New York restaurant stop serving balut?" Rappler.com, April 10. Available online: https://www.rappler.com/move-ph/balikbayan/89546-new-york-city-restaurant-balut-ban-petition (accessed July 20, 2018).

Raspa, R. (1984), "Exotic Foods among Italian Americans in Mormon Utah: Food as Nostalgic Enactment of Identity," in L. K. Brown and K. Mussell (eds), *Ethnic and Regional Foodways in the United States: The Performance of Group Identity*, 185–194, Knoxville: University of Tennessee.

Ratzel, F. (1896–1898), *The History of Mankind*, Vol. 1 of 3, London: Macmillan.

Ray, K. (2016), *The Ethnic Restaurateur*, London and New York: Bloomsbury.

Ray, K. (2018), "Suffering and Social Theory: Towards an Epistemology of Pleasure and Joy," Presidential Address, Association for the Study of Food and Society, Madison, Wisconsin, June 16, 2018.

Reinecke, J. E. (1996), *The Filipino Piecemeal Sugar Strike of 1924–1925*, Honolulu: Social Science Research Institute, University of Hawai'i.

Renner, H. D. (1944), *The Origin of Food Habits*, London: Faber & Faber Ltd.

Reyes-Estrope, C. (2017), "'Balut to Cost More after Lifting of Ban on Duck Egg Transport', Producers Say," *Philippine Daily Inquirer*, August 25. Available online: http://newsinfo.inquirer.net/925441/balut-to-cost-more-after-lifting-of-ban-on-duck-egg-transport-producers-say#ixzz4tEIFdygq (accessed September 10, 2017).

Roberts, E. (1837), *Embassy to the Eastern Courts of Cochin-China, Siam, and Muscat*, New York: Harper & Brothers. Available online: https://www.wdl.org/en/item/7317 (accessed May 28, 2017).

Ross, D. (2017), "Survivor: 35 Former Players Share Their Most Painful Memories," *Entertainment Weekly*, November 7. Available online: http://ew.com/tv/survivor-painful-moments-gallery/#malcolm-freberg-season-25-survivor-philippines-season-26-survivor-caramoan-fans-vs-favorites-season-34-survivor-game-changers (accessed May 22, 2018).

Ross, D. (2018), "Survivor: Jeff Probst Names the Most Disgusting Food Challenge Dish Ever," *Entertainment Weekly*, April 19. Available online: http://ew.com/tv/2018/04/19/survivor-jeff-probst-ghost-island-episode-9-balut (accessed May 22, 2018).

Rubin, L. C. (2008), "Beyond Bread and Circuses: Professional Competitive Eating," in L. C. Rubin (ed.), *Food for Thought. Essays on Eating and Culture*, 248–263, Jefferson, North Carolina: McFarland & Company, Inc.

Said, E. (1978), *Orientalism*, New York: Random House.

Santino, J. (1994), *Halloween and Other Festivals of Death and Life*, Knoxville: University of Tennessee Press.

Scattergood, A. (2017), "At Rice Bar, the Chef Is Cooking a Different Adobo Dish Every Week for a Year," *Los Angeles Times*, May 16. Available online: http://www.latimes.com/food/dailydish/la-fo-adobo-filipino-food-ricebar-20170423-htmlstory.html (accessed January 30, 2018).

Scott, W. H. (1989), *Filipinos in China before 1500*, Manila: De La Salle University Press.

Shah, A. (2014), "A Filipino Restaurant Owner Says Shame May Be One Reason Filipino Food Has Not Become Mainstream," PRI's The World, February 13, Available online: https://www.pri.org/stories/2014-02-13/according-filipino-restaurant-founder-new-yorkers-can-handle-plate-duck-embryos (accessed January 20, 2018).

Shaw, A. and L. H. Francia (eds) (2002), *Vestiges of War: The Philippine-American War and the Aftermath of an Imperial Dream 1899–1999*, New York: New York University Press.

Simoons, F. J. (1961), *Eat Not This Flesh: Food Avoidances in the Old World*, Madison: University of Wisconsin Press.

Spiers, K. (2017), "Oinkster Founder Andre Guerrero Helped Spread Filipino Flavors to the Masses," May 3. Available online: http://www.laweekly.com/restaurants/oinkster-founder-andre-guerrero-introduced-filipino-flavors-to-eagle-rock-8174628 (accessed June 4, 2017).

Staub, S. (1989), *Yemenis in New York City. The Folklore of Ethnicity*, Philadelphia: The Balch Institute Press.

Stromberg, Joseph (2012), "Why Does the Durian Fruit Smell So Terrible?" Smithsonian.com, November 30. Available online: https://www.smithsonianmag.com/science-nature/why-does-the-durian-fruit-smell-so-terrible-149205532/#Qtilx27RzUlPqypi.99 (accessed February 2, 2019).

Sumpter, K. C. (2015), "Masculinity and Meat Consumption: An Analysis through the Theoretical Lens of Hegemonic Masculinity and Alternative Masculinity Theories," *Sociology Compass*, 9 (2): 104–114.

Sydow, C. W. von (1977), "On the Spread of Tradition," in C. W. von Sydow (ed.), *Selected Papers on Folklore*, 44–59, New York: Arno Press.

Tadiar, N. X. M. (2009), *Things Fall Away: Philippine Historical Experience and the Makings of Globalization*, Durham, NC and London: Duke University Press.

Tagala, D. (2015), "U.S. Filipino Food Fans Say Balut Is Here to Stay," *Balitang America*, April 23. Available online: https://www.balitangamerica.tv/u-s-filipino-food-fans-say-balut-is-here-to-stay (accessed February 2, 2017).

Takaki, Ronald (1989), *Strangers from a Different Shore: A History of Asian Americans*. Penguin Books.

Theophano, J. (1982), "'It's Really Tomato Sauce but We Call It Gravy': A Study of Food and Women's Work among Italian-American Families," dissertation, University of Pennsylvania.

Theophano, J. (1991), "'I Gave Him a Cake:' An Interpretation of Two Italian-American Weddings," in S. Stern and J. Cicala (eds), *Creative Ethnicity*, 44–54, Logan: Utah State University.

Turner, V. (1967), "Betwixt and Between: The Liminal Period in Rites of Passage," in V. Turner (ed.), *The Forest of Symbols: Aspects of Ndembu Ritual*, 93–111, Ithaca, NY: Cornell University Press.

Turner, V. (1974), "Liminal to Liminoid, in Play, Flow, and Ritual: An Essay in Comparative Symbology," *Rice Institute Pamphlet – Rice University Studies*, 60 (3): 53–92.

United States Census Bureau (2012), "The Asian Population: 2010," 2010 Census Briefs. Issued March 2012. Available online: https://www.census.gov/prod/cen2010/briefs/c2010br-11.pdf (accessed May 15, 2017).

Urry, J. ([1990] 2002), *A Tourist Gaze*, London: Sage Publications.

Vadukul, A. (2012), "Sampling a Filipino Specialty They'll Be Competing to Gulp Down," *New York Times*, August 23. Available online: https://cityroom.blogs.nytimes.com/2012/08/23/sampling-a-filipino-dish-theyll-be-competing-to-gulp-down/?mtrref=www.google.com&gwh=693ACF5F2511E7F151B16CBAAED7655A&gwt=pay (accessed February 2, 2017).

Van Gennep, A. ([1909] 1965), *The Rites of Passage*, London: Routledge and Kegan.

Vardi, I. (2010), "Feeding Race: Eating Contests, the Black Body, and the Social Production of Group Boundaries through Amusement in Turn of the Twentieth Century America," *Food, Culture & Society*, 13 (3): 371–396.

Vick, M. (2016), "Manny Pacquiao Reveals What He Eats before a Big Fight," diply.com, August 18. Available online: https://diply.com/michael-vick/article/manny-pacquiao-pre-fight-diet (accessed May 23, 2017).

Visperas, E. (2005), "Lalaki Kinatay, Ininom ang Dugo," *Philstar Global*, March 16. Available online: https://www.philstar.com/probinsiya/2005/03/16/270604/lalaki-kinatay-ininom-ang-dugo (accessed May 23, 2017).

Walton, A. H. (1958), *Aphrodisiacs: From Legend to Prescription, a Study of Aphrodisiacs throughout the Ages, with Sections on Suitable Food, Glandular Extracts, Hormone Stimulation and Rejuvenation*, Westport, CT: Associated Booksellers.

Warde, A., L. Martens and W. Olsen (1999), "Consumption and the Problem of Variety: Cultural Omnivorousness, Social Distinction and Dining Out," *Sociology*, 33 (1): 105–127.

Weller, C. (2016), "Manila Is the Most Crowded City in the World—Here's What Life Is Like," *Business Insider*, August 4. Available online: https://www.businessinsider.com/manila-worlds-most-crowded-city-2016-8 (accessed January 2, 2019).

West, C. and D. H. Zimmerman (1987), "Doing Gender," *Gender and Society*, 1 (2): 125–151.

Williams-Forson, P. (2006), *Building Houses Out of Chicken Legs: Black Women, Food, and Power*, Chapel Hill: University of North Carolina.

Yoder, D. (1972), "Folk Cookery," in R. Dorson (ed.), *Folklore and Folklife: An Introduction*, 325–350, Chicago: University of Chicago Press.

Yoon, H. (2006), "What's in a Name? The Avocado Story," *National Public Radio*, July 19. Available online: https://www.npr.org/templates/story/story.php?storyId=5563805 (accessed March 21, 2017).

Yu, T. (2006), "Challenging the Politics of the 'Model Minority' Stereotype: A Case for Educational Equality," *Equity & Excellence in Education*, 39 (4): 325–333. Available online: https://doi.org/10.1080/10665680600932333 (accessed May 29, 2018).

Zembylas, M. (2013), "Affective Citizenship in Multicultural Societies: Implications for Critical Citizenship Education," *Citizenship Teaching and Learning*, 9 (1): 5–18.

Zhang, J. (2015), "Chinese American Culture in the Making: Perspectives and Reflections on Diasporic Folklore and Identity," *Journal of American Folklore*, 128 (510): 449–475.

Zhang, J. (2020), "Ethnic Genre and Folkloric Identity: Paradigm Shifts," *Western Folklore* 79 (1): pages forthcoming.

Zumwalt, R. (1988), *American Folklore Scholarship: A Dialogue of Dissent*, Bloomington: University of Indiana Press.

# Index